Wealth Creation
and Jobs

The Authors

David Sainsbury is Finance Director of J Sainsbury plc. He graduated from King's College, Cambridge where he read History and Psychology, and has an MBA degree from Columbia University in New York. He was a member of the Committee of Review of the Post Office (Carter Committee). He is a Governor of the London Business School.

Christopher Smallwood is Economics Editor of the Sunday Times. After teaching economics at Oxford and Edinburgh Universities in the early 1970's, he spent two years as an economic adviser to the Cabinet Office, and five years at the Treasury, where he was mainly involved with international monetary issues and the financing of the nationalised industries. In 1983 he joined BP as their Senior Economist in corporate planning, and was latterly responsible for financial strategy and planning.

The authors wish to acknowledge the contribution to this book made by Zahid Nawaz who arranged the computer simulations and who gave us other invaluable help. The opinions expressed in it, however, are solely the responsibility of the authors.

Wealth Creation and Jobs

David Sainsbury
Christopher Smallwood

Public Policy Centre/London

ISBN 0 948581 04 2

Published by the Public Policy Centre
Pollen House, 10–12 Cork Street, London W1X 1PD
01–437 8633

Phototypeset in Linotron 10/12 Trump Mediaeval
by Wyvern Typesetting Limited, Bristol

Printed in England by Blackrose Press,
29 Clerkenwell Close, London EC1

31·7 95 (D)

The Public Policy Centre

THE PUBLIC POLICY CENTRE is an independent charitable Trust. Its principal purpose is to bring fresh thinking to bear on the central economic, social and governmental questions of the day. Through a programme of research, education and publication, it aims to influence the climate of informed opinion, particularly among those responsible for deciding policy.

The Centre's approach is objective and non-partisan. It is concerned with practical policy issues, not with commissioning long-term projects of pure research. It aims to explore and develop the policy relevance of academic ideas.

The Trustees are responsible for the general supervision of the Centre's work. In selecting topics for study and deciding whether to publish a manuscript as a Centre publication, they are guided by the Centre's Advisory Board under the chairmanship of Dick Taverne QC.

Publications are subject to intensive prior discussion by an expert panel containing a blend of academic and practical experience. Responsibility for the contents remains, however, with the individual authors. Hence, the views expressed should be understood to be solely those of the authors and should not be attributed to the Centre, its Trustees, staff, members of the Advisory Board, or organizations and individuals providing financial support for the Centre's work.

Contents

Contents

Preface

Britain's industrial decline can be reversed—that is the main theme of this book. The trouble, as the authors David Sainsbury and Christopher Smallwood argue, has been, at least in part, a wrong sense of priorities in government. Good macro-economic management has always been regarded as the key to national success. A strategy for industry, when it has featured at all in the national agenda, has tended to come under Any Other Business. But if we are to reduce unemployment substantially, we need to have a better balance between macro-policies and policies to speed up the process of industrial change. If the performance of British industry does not improve, macro-economic policy alone cannot solve our problems.

The case they make is a convincing one. If we look at a comparison with our more successful competitors, like Japan or Germany, their success seems to owe less to better macro-economic management than to higher productivity and a greater adaptability of their industries for technological change. Possibly the most telling point in the book is made by the two "diamond" diagrams on pages 33 and 34 in Chapter 2, showing how dramatically Japanese industry changed between 1959 and 1985, from a labour-intensive to a knowledge-intensive structure and how little change there has been in Britain.

If we developed an effective strategy for industry which only modestly improved productivity and exports, the gains would be striking. The task of macro-economic management which now faces almost insuperable obstacles, would be greatly eased.

Expansion would not lead almost immediately to inflation and balance of payments crises. There would be a substantial improvement in jobs, to some extent in exporting companies and those competing with imports, but also more generally because a more successful industry could be the basis for increased public spending with its greatly beneficial effects on employment.

Unfortunately "industrial policy" has in many circles acquired a bad name. Industrial leaders who acknowledge that government can play an important role in improving industrial performance, shy away from the idea of industrial policy because they fear it means government telling them how to run their companies. Past Labour governments have identified it with "picking winners", helping some companies at the expense of others. But no government can avoid an involvement in areas which directly impinge on the performance of industry, though Mrs. Thatcher has pretended that it can. In reality the only question is what priority is given to the needs of industry and whether policies in these areas hinder or speed up the process of industrial change.

Such policies, the book argues, imply a positive and a negative role for government. The negative consists of removing the obstacles that stop markets working effectively, such as disincentives and inefficient regulations. But at least equally important is the positive role—making certain that people have the education and skills to get jobs, aligning the resources that go into Research and Development with industrial priorities, and ensuring that the financial markets meet industry's long term needs.

In our view the importance of this book lies partly in the detailed proposals for reform, which we believe would enable a substantial advance to be made in economic growth: but most of all in its potential impact on our sense of economic priorities. Economic policy-makers should become at least as concerned about the changing trends in world markets, and the extent to which our industry is adapting to them, as they are about trends in the balance of payments, the public sector borrowing requirement and the monetary aggregates.

The aim of the authors is far more ambitious than promoting particular remedies for particular aspects of our industrial malaise. They want to change the terms of the political and economic debate.

DICK TAVERNE QC, *Advisory Board Chairman*
ROGER LIDDLE, *Director*

CHAPTER 1

Wealth Creation and Jobs

It was James Callaghan who in 1976 declared that the proposition that governments could spend their way to full employment had been "tested to destruction". Inflation exceeded 20 per cent, the balance of payments was in massive deficit, and officials of the International Monetary Fund were installed at the Treasury. The era of Keynesian economics which had dominated British economic policy since the war had come to an end, and the age of monetarism was about to dawn.

Ten years later, simple Keynesianism as summarised by Callaghan remains discredited, but the much proclaimed monetarist alternative is languishing in the same state. No-one believes any more that governments can simply spend their way out of unemployment, but it is equally clear that the economies and particularly the labour markets of the West European countries have not shown the tendency to "equilibrate" postulated by the monetarist theories, and that the promised road to non-inflationary growth at full employment has equally proved to be a blind alley.

It has been amply demonstrated that the maintenance of sensible monetary and other macro-economic policies is not alone sufficient to produce a phoenix from the ashes: the new macro-economic policies have proved as incapable as those they supplanted of enabling the economy to achieve its productive potential, and bringing aggregate demand and supply into balance without undue inflation at full employment. But if Keynesian expansionary policies were constrained by an inflationary barrier, policies of monetary restraint have equally

1

foundered on the rigidity of the labour markets which have prevented a recovery in employment as inflation has come down. The combination of low inflation and chronically high unemployment which these policies have produced is—to say the least—no more impressive than the results produced by the policies in operation until the mid 70's.

This is true not only for Britain, but for Western Europe as a whole. Employment projections recently produced by the International Monetary Fund suggest that unemployment in Western Europe may fall by some 1 per cent by 1991. The London Business School's latest economic forecast (Economic Outlook, Autumn 1986), foresees no significant fall in unemployment in Britain by the end of the decade, beyond that attributable to government special employment schemes. Unemployment in Britain has been on a rising trend for most of the last seven years, and whilst the trend may now be levelling off, there is no convincing evidence that without an entirely fresh approach to economic policy unemployment can be substantially reduced.

The central contention of this book is that the main focus of economic policy—and of the efforts of the army of policy-makers in government departments attempting to improve the performance of the economy—should urgently be shifted away from obsessive concentration on macro-economic aggregates to more directly-targeted methods of improving the process of wealth creation itself. This is not to say that demand management and monetary control are without importance: indeed, it is vitally necessary to keep monetary and fiscal policies in proper balance. But rather that it is only through the design and application of a range of policies specifically developed to raise the performance of industry that a return to non-inflationary growth at high levels of employment is likely to be achieved. What, for want of a better phrase, we have called "industrial policy" needs to be brought to the centre of the stage.

This book argues that policies aimed directly at assisting industry to compete more successfully in international markets are required not only to raise the rate of growth, and hence permit the improvements in schools, hospitals and social services which are now a matter of urgency, but also to enable the "inflation barrier" to be pushed back as output expands and hence permit a return to something more like full employment to take place.

"Industrial policy" is often discussed in micro-economic terms—correcting market failures of one type or another. There is also, however, a powerful macro-economic case, in terms of employment, inflation and growth, for the determined pursuit of measures aimed at improving the performance of industry in international markets. The macro-economic case for industrial policy is as yet largely undeveloped, and the purpose of this first chapter is to explain the inter-relationship between industrial policy and macro-economic policies of the more traditional type, and the mechanisms by which industrial policies can make a vital contribution to the reconciliation of price stability with full employment.

The macro-economic case for industrial policy emerges from the experience of the British economy and to some extent of other European economies over the last 20 years.

The Keynesian Record

The historian A. J. P. Taylor once said that in the 1920's and 1930's—the last period when there was an unemployment crisis—mass unemployment was a mystery to economic theorists: they had no effective prescription to offer until Keynes came along and said that the way to cure the unemployment problem was to give people jobs.

Most of the current generation of policy makers were educated in Keynesian economics and for a long period after the war the policies they applied were astonishingly successful. Full employment was achieved through budgetary policy, essentially by increasing public spending or lowering taxation when activity turned down and doing the reverse when the economy "overheated" and inflation appeared. Until the mid-1960's full employment was maintained and the international economy enjoyed an unparalleled period of rapid non-inflationary growth. Much to the chagrin of the ultra-left, Keynes appeared to have solved the main problems of capitalism.

From the mid-1960's, however, inflation began to creep up, not just in Britain but throughout the industrialised world. And

3

as it did so the trend unemployment rate also began to rise: at each phase of each succeeding cycle, inflation was higher and employment was lower than it had been in the previous one. A number of explanations were put forward for this phenomenon. One was the increase in spending and world money supply associated with the prosecution of the Vietnam war in the late 1960's. Another was the simultaneous expansion of all major industrialised economies in the early 1970's which put unsustainable pressure on world commodity prices. Since 45 per cent of the organisation for Economic Co-operation and Development's (OECD) imports consist of commodities, the explosion in world commodity prices which took place in those years caused inflation to rise rapidly throughout the industrialised world. Thirdly, the abandonment of the dollar–gold exchange standard at the beginning of the 1970's and then of any attempt to maintain exchange rate stability in the wake of the 1973 oil crisis removed a major source of discipline on policy makers and enabled expansionary or even profligate policies to be pursued far longer than would otherwise have been possible. And there had always been the feeling that the maintenance of high growth and full employment for the 20 years following the war had been something of a miracle. Keynes had written in the early 1940's of the need for arrangements to restrain pay and price increases if the full employment policies he advocated were implemented. In retrospect it is remarkable that the pressure of demand could have been sustained for so long without an inflationary explosion or effective institutional arrangements for regulating pay and price rises.

In any event, by the early 1970's it had become clear that full employment could only be maintained without unacceptable inflation within the framework of a robust incomes policy. When Edward Heath's tightly defined statutory policy was blown apart by the miners' strike in the winter of 1973 and his defeat in the General Election of February 1974, the new Labour government attempted to maintain a high level of employment without a defined incomes policy. The result was a rapid acceleration in the inflation rate, driven by escalating pay claims, up towards 30 per cent. The process was finally called to a halt by the most draconian incomes policy so far devised—a single rise of £6 per week for every employee in the country, except for those earning over £8,500 per year who were required to forego any pay increase at all.

The years 1976–79 were the years of incomes policy "par excellence". The original £6 per week norm was made somewhat more flexible in succeeding years to allow a limited restoration of differentials. The government sought to get across the message that it could no longer be expected simply to spend money to maintain full employment without thought for the inflationary consequences, and that a high level of employment could be maintained only within the context of pay restraint and a manageable inflation rate. The Callaghan–Healey incomes policies were remarkably successful, with inflation slowing down and growth recovering right up to the infamous "winter of discontent" in 1979 when public sector groups in particular refused to accept the 5 per cent limit promulgated by the government, and a wave of strikes left the rubbish uncollected and the dead unburied.

Before the "winter of discontent" it had become received wisdom that an effective incomes policy was vital for the success of the British economy. Indeed, long before Mrs. Thatcher used the phrase, James Callaghan claimed "that there was no alternative" to the policy combination being pursued by the Labour government. The power of the unions was such, and the need to manage wage claims appeared to be so essential, that the Conservative victory in June 1979 produced a fall in the stock market. Yet it was soon widely accepted that centralised incomes policies had finally failed, and that the economy needed to be run in another way.

The Monetarist Experiment

The new Conservative government was in no position to construct incomes policies of the Callaghan–Healey type in any case, since they relied essentially on the relationship between the Labour government and the Trade Union movement. Nor was it realistic to try to return to statutory incomes policies of the Heath type: few believed that they could be sustained against a hostile union movement, and they were anathema to the Prime Minister and her leading supporters in the Government. Instead the government chose to adopt what was billed as a wholly new approach to the management of the economy, summed up in the word "monetarism". They launched what came to be known as the "monetarist experiment" and overseas observers sat back with astonishment and some admiration to see what would be the outcome for "greenhouse Britain".

The importance of effective control of the money supply was not a new idea. It had been stressed by Denis Healey during his years as Chancellor, and it had a long and respectable lineage in economic theory, going back at least to David Hume in the middle of the 18th century. Ambitious claims were, however, made about the extent to which monetary policy, properly pursued, could resolve many of the economic problems facing Britain, producing not only price stability but a resurgence of growth and full employment. Monetarist economics had become fashionable through the constant advocacy of Professor Milton Friedman, and the doctrine was extremely convenient in political terms since it enabled the Conservative government to adopt an intellectually respectable policy without having to deal with over-mighty union barons. In line with the tenets of the theories which were then fashionable, the new government devised and announced a "medium-term financial strategy", embodying a steady planned reduction in monetary growth over a number of years and parallel reductions in government borrowing. The new Financial Secretary to the Treasury, Nigel Lawson, argued that "intermediate targets" such as the money supply were within the government's control whereas "final targets" such as the rate of inflation or the level of employment were not.

The theoretical rationale for the policy was that when the markets and those making pay bargains realised that the government was prepared to do whatever was necessary to restrain the growth of the money supply within the targets which had been declared—i.e. whatever the cost in lost production and jobs—inflationary expectations would be broken. As the rate of unemployment rose above the so-called "natural rate"—i.e. the rate at which inflation ceased to accelerate—the rate of pay settlements would fall steadily bringing inflation tumbling in its wake. This process would go on as long as the excess supply of labour persisted, so that if the government, having brought the money supply under control, thereafter allowed it to grow at a steady rate, the growing money supply would increasingly produce higher output rather than higher prices. If for example the government planned that the money supply should grow by 6 per cent and inflation was 3 per cent, that monetary policy would be consistent with 3 per cent growth of real output in the economy. If then the following year the rate of inflation decelerated to 2 per cent but the policy of 6 per cent monetary growth were maintained the real growth of the economy would rise to 4 per cent.

Hence the claim which was so paradoxical to Keynesian ears that restrictive policies would in the end lead to non-inflationary growth and a recovery in employment. Indeed, the more extreme advocates of the new policy claimed that deceleration and then steady control of the money supply was all that was required, given time, for inflation to be defeated, growth to be resumed, and full employment to be restored. In their view once the bubble of inflationary expectations was pricked an "equilibrating process" would operate quite rapidly: after a short sharp recession the economy would bounce back strongly and unemployment fall back.

These expectations have not been fulfilled. The truth of Keynes' charge in the circumstances of 1936 that "the characteristics of the classical theory happen not to be those of the economic society in which we actually live, with the result that its teaching is misleading and disastrous if we attempt to apply it to the facts of experience", have been shown to apply with equal force to the cruder forms of monetarist doctrine. In particular, the labour markets have simply not behaved in the way the theory postulated, either in Britain or in the other European industrialised countries. In Britain, although unemployment has risen to levels unimaginable ten years ago and has continued to rise remorselessly until recently, wages at no time led prices down. Indeed there has been no significant fall in earnings growth since 1982. The theoretical mechanisms by which growth should resume at a sufficient rate to restore full employment has not operated in the world as it actually exists. True, inflation has fallen, and growth has resumed at a modest rate, but the economy appears at best to have made a step change to a chronically high level of unemployment, which shows no sign of coming down except as the result not of the working of markets, but of government special employment schemes. If the productive potential of the economy is to be achieved and then raised, at a high level of employment, it is clear that policies in addition to tight money and prudent budgeting are required, though continued monetary control will be necessary to make sure that the required improvement in performance takes place in non-inflationary conditions.

The Need for a New Approach

Reviewing the experience of the last 20 years from the failure of straight Keynesian policies through the experience with Keynesian plus incomes policies and finally the years of the monetarist experiment, a number of important lessons can be drawn.

First, it is true as James Callaghan said that governments cannot simply spend their way out of unemployment. A "dash for growth", which in the 1950's and 1960's during the era of fixed exchange rates would produce a balance of payments and sterling crisis, in these days of flexible exchange rates rapidly leads to accelerating inflation. About 30 per cent of spending in Britain goes on imports, and the marginal propensity to import exceeds 50 per cent. So a sizeable boost to spending is soon associated with a cascade of imports and a sinking exchange rate. Rising import prices feed through to the general price level producing higher wages claims and an accelerating inflationary spiral which sooner or later requires the expansion to be halted.

Secondly, however, it has been demonstrated that the labour market does not "equilibrate" in the way suggested by the doctrines of monetarism. Our experience has been that the economy does not automatically return to full employment and non-inflationary growth following a period of monetary deceleration. If Keynesian attacks on British economic problems have ultimately wasted themselves in inflation, the monetarist assault has no answer to high and continuing unemployment.

Thirdly, although incomes policies can be effective in restraining wage inflation for a while, they are most effective in the short term and as time goes on they become harder to sustain. They hinder the process of resource allocation which in

8

turn leads to a steady build up of wage pressures in particular parts of the economy. It may be possible in future to design incomes policies (such as the varieties of tax based incomes policy which have been suggested) which succeed in exerting a restraining influence over pay rises without at the end of the day being so rigid that they are blown apart. There is certainly a case for incomes policies of this type when, as at present, a short term step change in the level of activity and employment needs to be contrived. But incomes policies do not hold the key to improving the long-term performance of the economy on which the level of prosperity and employment ultimately depend.

It is noticeable that the industrial economies which have enjoyed outstanding success over this period—Japan and Germany—have been characterised by strong export-orientated industries, increasing their share of world markets, and *rising* exchange rates as a result of strong export performance which have made an important contribution to price stability in the two countries. The spirit of the approach recommended in this book is that the government should mobilise and co-ordinate all its resources so as to help industry advance in international markets, thus enabling a firm or rising exchange rate to be maintained along with enhanced growth and minimal inflation. Britain should seek to emulate its most successful competitors, but in view of the relative weakness of British industry, improved competitiveness will require the development and implementation of public policies specifically designed for the purpose.

The Role of Industrial Policy

The macro-economic role of industrial policy can be illustrated with the help of Diagram I, which relates the price level to the level of output in the economy (and assumes that employment is basically a function of output). The traditional Keynesian view of demand–inflation is represented by the line OK. According to this view, as long as there is significant excess capacity in industry and a margin of unemployment, spending can be increased and output expanded without any significant increase in the price level. However, as demand rises to the limits of industrial capacity and towards the full employment point, prices will start to rise and will continue to do so until the excess demand is choked off. In order to control inflation in these circumstances, it is appropriate for the government to restrain spending and reduce the money supply.

DIAGRAM I

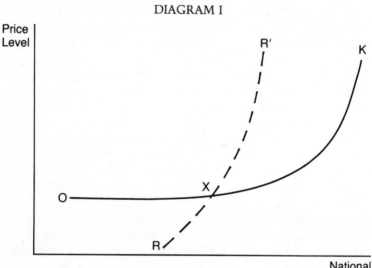

This view fitted the "facts of experience" quite well for the 20 years following the war, when a fairly stable relationship (known as the Phillips curve) between the level of unemployment and the rate of increase of prices was observed in the region of full employment for most industrial economies. This was also a period, of course, in which exchange rates remained largely fixed.

The position the economy currently finds itself in, however, is illustrated by the point X on the line RR'. It is operating well below the full employment level of output and with a flexible exchange rate. This means that any attempt to expand spending, financed by an increase in the public sector borrowing requirement (PSBR), or in the rate of growth of the money supply, will rapidly produce an acceleration of inflation. The exchange rate will quickly respond, pushing up import prices and triggering off the familiar wage–price spiral, so that instead of proceeding from X along the line OK as in a closed economy, or an economy with a stable exchange rate, it follows a path along RR'. The exchange rate response will be more severe to the extent that the initial downturn resulted in a loss of industrial capacity. Expansion back to full employment by the traditional means is then effectively blocked by an "inflation barrier".

Once an economy, like the British economy, makes a step change downwards in its *level* of activity and employment, and arrives at a point like X, it is clear that it becomes exceedingly difficult by use of the traditional policy instruments to make a similar step change back again. Growth may resume, roughly in line with the increasing productive potential of the economy, but an attempt to achieve growth at the "unsustainable" rates required to restore full employment by expanding demand cannot be maintained. The point X is arbitrarily chosen: depending on the levels to which unemployment departs from the full employment point, the higher it is likely to remain. Hence the British economy, and to a lesser degree the other West European economies, are "locked in" to high unemployment levels, and the prescriptions of economic theory—whether Keynesian or monetarist—are unable to resolve the problem.

The picture of the predicament the British economy finds itself in, represented by the line RR', is not merely a theoretical speculation. Most econometric models embody the view that in relatively open economies, such as Britain and most of the West European economies, expansionary policies generate inflation via a fall in the exchange rate as explained above. The results of simulations carried out by the London Business School to test the theoretical propositions contained in this chapter bear out to a considerable degree the relative slopes of the lines OK and RR' shown in the diagram. The results are set out and discussed in detail in Chapter 5. The conclusion which naturally follows is that it is necessary to contrive a form of expansion which avoids a collapse of the exchange rate. If this can be achieved, it should be possible to expand a long way (in terms of the diagram along OK instead of RR') without inflation reaching unacceptable levels.

It is interesting in this respect to note that America's "great leap forward" from record unemployment levels to today's relatively low level of around 7 per cent, took place because a large increase in the federal deficit (a huge increase in public spending, particularly on defence, and some tax cuts) was accompanied by a *rise* in the value of the dollar on the foreign exchanges. Fortunately, when the dollar began to fall, falling world commodity prices negated the impact of this on inflation in the United States. America therefore managed to expand along OK instead of RR', and it did this by keeping interest rates *high*, whilst expanding the budget deficit, to pull in foreign capital and support the dollar that way. It has therefore managed to "step back" to a higher employment level, though at the cost, of course, of a massive and unsustainable trade deficit.

There is nothing peculiar about the American economy in this respect: the same is likely also to hold for most of the Western industrialised economies. There is mounting evidence that the inflationary process is not primarily transmitted directly from spending or money supply increases to wage and price rises, but via changes in the exchange rate and increases in world commodity prices. Changes in import prices lead to rising pay claims, and the two in turn cause the general rate of inflation to go up across an industrial economy. Michael Bruno, Head of the Israeli Central Bank, in his book "The Economics of Worldwide Stagflation", has identified "the dominant influence of exchange rates and import prices on inflation", and this appears to be true for most European countries as well as the United States.

The main question therefore is whether Britain can develop and implement policies enabling it to emulate the American achievement, generating an increased rate of expansion in combination with exchange rate stability, though without running into balance of payments deficits which in Britain's case it would be impossible to sustain. This would enable us to achieve the "step back" which is required for a high employment level to be restored without soaring inflation.

Alternative Ways Forward

Four different types of policy, not all mutually exclusive, have been suggested in order to try to achieve this type of result.

Firstly, the British government could seek to copy directly the successful American policy combination, by increasing and expanding the PSBR, but at the same time maintaining monetary restraint and keeping interest rates high in order to avoid a slide in the exchange rate. This is the type of policy advocated by the Employment Institute, and given the lack of sensitivity of pay settlements in Britain to changes in unemployment, as evidenced by the experience of the last four years, it might indeed be possible to step up to a higher employment level for a time, without more inflation, if exchange rate stability could be sustained in this way.

Secondly, there is the Labour Party's approach based on induced capital repatriation. Labour has proposed removing the tax privileges from financial institutions—insurance companies and pension funds—which fail to repatriate most of their overseas investments and invest the money instead in bonds of a proposed new National Investment Bank. As Roy Hattersley has said "The next Labour government, running a high employment economy, will have to risk additional imports producing further depreciation. The more that pressure can be relieved by the repatriation of capital scheme, the less need there will be for other measures." This then provides an alternative to the high interest rate policy as a means of inducing capital inflow sufficient to fund the current account deficit on the balance of payments which would be generated by a higher level of spending. This type of approach therefore belongs in the same framework of thought—attempting to combine expansion with exchange rate stability. Simulations on the Treasury model carried out by the ITEM Club demonstrated that if a regular capital inflow was achieved by Labour's policies, the economy could expand quite a long way back towards full employment without very much more inflation.[1]

The third approach is a joint expansion co-ordinated by the major industrial economies. As explained above, if one country alone attempts to expand the expansion is aborted as its exchange rate drops and inflation accelerates. This has been the British experience repeatedly since the war, and the same phenomenon was observed when Mitterand attempted to

---

1 Available from the authors on request.

expand the French economy unilaterally from 1981. If, however, the increase in spending in one country is matched by expansionary measures taken by its main trading partners, and the policies are co-ordinated so that the increase in imports associated with the higher level of activity in each country is matched by an increase in exports to its trading partners, the initial set of exchange rates can on this account remain unchanged and the generation of inflation from this source can be avoided. Such a co-ordinated expansion could, for example, be contrived by the members of the European Community, within the context of the European Monetary System (EMS).

This type of process occurred spontaneously through most of the 20 year period following the war when the major industrial economies expanded together within the context of a system of fixed exchange rates. The advocates of co-ordinated expansion claim that it is now desirable to restart a similar process with some co-ordinated pump-priming, and that as long as exchange rates did not move it would again be possible for expansion to take place without running into the inflationary barrier which would stop any one country acting alone. This process could indeed continue until rising demand had its impact on world commodity markets and import prices began to rise from that source.

Fourthly, the government could devise and implement a series of measures aimed at raising the performance of British industry and improving its competitiveness in international markets. A successful industrial policy with these objectives would raise the rate of growth of exports, and diminish the propensity to import as domestic industry succeeded in replacing the products of foreign competitors in British markets. Expansion associated with an improvement in competitiveness generates balance of payments *strength* rather than weakness and a tendency for the exchange rate to *rise*. This is a policy aimed at causing the British economy to emulate those of Germany and Japan, rather than the United States, since the growth and prosperity of the former two economies have been built on the advance of their industries in world markets. Their rising exchange rates have been generated by industrial success and have made a continuing contribution to price stability, thus helping to produce a virtuous circle of improving competitiveness and trading success. Moreover, a steady improvement in the competitiveness of British industry would give the Government more freedom of manoeuvre in economic policy. Not only would it result in the direct creation of more jobs, it would also enable governments to increase domestic spending either through increased public expenditure programmes or tax cuts, without a slide in the exchange rate. It would therefore create the conditions in which a high level of employment in the economy could be restored without unacceptable inflation.

Which of these four different types of policy is likely to be most effective?

The American combination of large budget deficits, tight money and high interest rates is not readily transferable to Britain. The dollar is the major international reserve currency and benefits from the confidence of investors in the strength of the United States economy. Neither of these considerations applies to sterling. In the event of a major expansion of the public sector borrowing requirement, higher interest rates—at least at levels which would be tolerable to the domestic community—are unlikely in themselves to be sufficient to sustain sterling on the foreign exchanges. Moreover, as is becoming increasingly clear in the American case, the large trade deficits associated with large budget deficits are not sustainable indefinitely. It may be difficult to maintain high employment when the necessary corrections eventually take place. And when the exchange rate finally does fall, this will produce a sharp cut in living standards. Finally, real interest rates are already at record levels in the United Kingdom and exert an adverse effect on the rate of investment. Markedly higher real interest rates could be extremely damaging to investment and hence to growth in the longer-term.

One of the worries about Labour's approach is: what happens when the capital has been repatriated? Presumably the country is then left with a massive deficit on the current account of the balance of payments and without the funds to finance it. Looked at in this way, capital repatriation appears as a device merely to defer the inevitable sterling and inflation crisis, unless the breathing space, which the capital inflow would provide, is used to improve the competitiveness of British industry. Competitiveness would need to improve sufficiently to ensure that, as the capital inflow diminishes, export performance improved and the propensity to import fell to the extent necessary to remove the current account deficit. Labour's capital repatriation policy does not therefore avoid the need for a successful industrial policy: the long term success of Labour's whole approach positively requires this.

A more fundamental worry is that foreign investors in Britain, anticipating the sterling and inflation crisis to come as the trade deficit rises, will withdraw their capital and stop investing in Britain. In these circumstances the capital inflow caused by the repatriation of British funds may be matched by reduced capital inflow from other sources and capital flight. Labour's capital repatriation policy would not then create additional scope to expand the economy without a fall in the exchange rate, even in the short-term.

If a co-ordinated expansion in Europe could be contrived, this might indeed enable growth to be stepped up and unemployment brought down without a serious rise in inflation. This is illustrated by computer simulations, specially commissioned from the London Business School, the results of which are set out in Chapter 5. But the political difficulties standing in the way of such an agreement are formidable. A joint *fiscal* expansion—whether it involved increases in spending or reductions in taxation in each of the participating countries— would require an agreement impinging on areas of the greatest political sensitivity. This degree of co-ordination has never previously been achieved, although it was partially approached at the Bonn Economic Summit in 1978. A joint *monetary* expansion (co-ordinated cuts in interest rates) may be more realistic, and could also be consistent with unchanged exchange rates, but it would be less effective than fiscal action, precisely because the main expansionary effect of a stimulatory monetary policy, in the case of an individual country, comes through the exchange rate depreciation with which it is generally associated. Co-ordinated expansion in Europe remains a worthwhile aim which could deliver significant benefits—particularly within the context of the exchange rate mechanism of the EMS—but there should be no illusions about the difficulties of getting such an approach implemented.

We are left therefore with the "industrial policy" approach—

the development and implementation of a set of policies designed to raise the performance of industry, improve price and non-price competitiveness, and by strengthening the balance of trade create a context within which expansionary policies could be pursued without generating an inflationary explosion. This route has the advantage over co-ordinated expansion that it is not dependent on the agreement of other countries. And a successful industrial policy, far from damaging the prospects for long-term growth—the danger of trying to follow the American example—removes the balance of payments constraint and pushes back the inflationary barrier to full employment by *improving* industrial performance and growth. A determined effort to formulate and implement "industrial policies" aimed at helping British industry advance in world markets therefore offers the best hope of creating the conditions for non-inflationary growth at a sufficient rate to allow a high level of employment to be achieved once again.

What Sort of Industrial Policy?

The macro-economic rationale for industrial policy is thus two-fold. First, it aims to raise the growth of value-added or productivity, and hence the underlying growth rate of the economy in the long-term. If productivity in Britain grows more slowly than in our main competitors, this means, *ceteris paribus*, that foreign goods gradually become cheaper—or achieve better quality for the same price—than British goods, leading to a deterioration in the British balance of trade, which requires in turn a depreciation of sterling and hence a cut in living standards in Britain to restore balance. This is one of the principal elements—together with the chronic tendency of British industry to pay high nominal wage increases—in the economic story of Britain since the war. The different macro-economic policies which have been pursued have constituted a continual rearguard action—adjusting the pound downwards, and deflating and/or imposing incomes policies not just to regulate inflation but to produce the cut in real income needed to re-balance the economy in the wake of industrial failure. British industry's lack of competitive success has been a root

17

cause of the country's chronic tendency to balance of payments weakness over the past 30 years, of the sliding real exchange rate, and hence of the tendency for inflation here to be worse than in many of our competitor countries. Equally, to reverse these trends a sustained improvement in industry's perform- ance is a fundamental requirement.

Secondly, to the extent that industrial policy succeeds in raising the competitiveness of British industry in international markets and creates a tendency for the exchange rate to *rise*, it can establish conditions in which expansionary policies of the Keynesian type can also be pursued to bring unemployment down without generating unacceptable inflation. In terms of Diagram I (page 10) the combination of an industrial policy to improve competitiveness and Keynesian policies to increase spending should enable the economy to expand towards full employment along the path OK, or some path beneath this as the economy's capacity to supply products is improved. The contention of this book is that the two types of policy *in combination* offer the way out of the low productivity/high unemployment/inflationary society Britain has become.

When we talk about wealth creation, and the ability of British industry to compete in world markets, we are, of course, referring both to manufactured goods and to services. While there has been much political debate about the relative merits of service industries and manufacturing industries, it makes no difference in which we achieve and maintain a competitive advantage. Manufacturing is not inherently a more virtuous activity. A look at Britain's trade statistics, however, makes it clear that, in the timescale relevant to public policies, we will have to rely on having a substantial and successful manufactur- ing sector. World trade in goods is four times as great as the world trade in services, and over the period 1968–1983 both markets grew at the same average annual rate of $11\frac{1}{4}$ per cent (Bank of England Quarterly Bulletin, September 1985). Britain would, therefore, have to perform extraordinarily well in services to compensate for abandoning a large manufacturing sector.

Secondly, the UK share of world trade in services has been falling as sharply over the last 15 years as our share of manu- factured goods. A disastrous loss of market share in shipping was a major cause, but our share of exports of financial services and consultancy slumped from 14 to 8 per cent, while in computer software, where we pride ourselves on excellence, we have been losing out in world markets to the Americans and French. Britain is also going to find it very difficult to compete in the future in financial services against the Americans and the Japanese. Japan in particular has built up enormous strength in financial services on the back of its huge trade surplus, and British financial service companies will have to devise very sophisticated strategies to be able to compete against them.

Thirdly, in both the USA and the UK the fastest growing sectors, as measured by employment trends, have been producer services, that is intermediate services such as consultancy, contracting and banking, where demand is governed by the output or investment decisions of companies. In other words, the fastest growing sector of services is one which is dependent on having a buoyant manufacturing industry.

When it comes to job creation on the other hand, we probably will have to rely very heavily on new service jobs. Because of productivity gains "jobless growth" may become a fact of life in manufacturing industry as it has been for several decades in agriculture. The scope for productivity gains in the supply of services is, however, much less than in manufacturing. Waiters are probably no more efficient today than a hundred years ago. The result is that while the share of services in total output has not grown as fast as some people think, the contribution of services to employment has been very large. The share of services in total UK employment rose from around 43 per cent in 1950 to nearly 65 per cent in 1985. If one compares the components of employment in the USA and the UK in 1961, and 1983, then it can be seen that in both countries, when the figures have been adjusted for population growth, all the growth of jobs in the period has been in the service sector. Thus while we cannot rely on the service sector to create all the wealth we need to preserve our relative standard of living, in order to bring down unemployment we must create the right climate for the service industries to grow and prosper.

If it is accepted that the ability of British industry to compete successfully in goods and services is the key constraint on expanding the economy, then there is a clear case for devoting substantial resources to improving the performance of industry. The case is the classic one in terms of "externalities". If it is true that increased competitive success can bring benefits to the wider economy in terms of a higher level of activity and employment, which individual producers cannot be expected to take into account in formulating their investment decisions and business strategies, then there is a clear case for public funds to be deployed in order to influence the decisions of private producers and enable the wider benefits of industrial success for the economy as a whole to be achieved. Indeed, to the extent that income is higher than would have been the case without the policy—as a result of higher productivity growth as well as the extra leeway successful industrial policies may provide for a higher level of domestic spending—the additional income can be thought of as constituting a stream of returns to the funds "invested" in the industrial programme.

How should such resources be used? In designing policies to raise the growth of productivity or value-added in the economy, it is helpful to recognise that economic growth arises from two distinct types of process;

i) improvements in the performance of existing industries or activities;

ii) the continuous transfer of resources from low to high productivity sectors.

The second is often overlooked. Yet policies which succeed in accelerating the transfer of resources to more productive areas of the economy may make an important contribution to raising the growth rate. Equally, other policies, such as those designed to reduce real wages, may have the effect of reducing the transfer of resources from labour-intensive low-productivity areas to more successful parts of the economy and thus lowering the growth rate. Such policies offer only temporary respite since we cannot in the long term compete with the Newly Industrialising Countries in terms of price. They essentially offer a trade-off between short-term improvements in the level of activity and reduced growth prospects. Short-term policies need to be designed which are consistent with longer-term economic objectives which will presumably include higher productivity and improved, rather than reduced, living standards. In order for this to happen, however, the trade-off has first to be recognised and defined. At present this is generally not the case because of the static short-term framework of most macro-economic policy analysis.

The industrial policies advocated in this book are designed to *accelerate* the responsiveness of the economy to changing market signals, enabling the present set of industries to respond more quickly and effectively to market developments, and enabling resources, both capital and labour, to shift more quickly and easily from the activities of the past to the activities of the future. The strategy recommended in this book does not therefore rest on central direction: it sets out to create a framework within which those taking part in the competitive struggle can compete more successfully.

The policies required to achieve this objective are set out in Chapters 2 to 4. They are far-reaching and encompass wide areas of public policy, from competition policy through tax and financing proposals to the entire system of education and training, and the targeting of technological resources. Chapter 5 displays the results of a series of computer simulations designed to explore the scale of benefits which could accrue to the economy if policies of the type proposed in this book were successfully implemented. The results confirm in a striking way the theoretical view presented in this chapter that a significant improvement in industry's competitiveness would create the conditions in which a high level of employment could be restored without the reappearance of inflation at unacceptable levels.

CHAPTER 2

New Dynamics of World Markets

The arguments for deploying resources to improve the competitiveness of industry are very powerful. Yet very little thought has been given in the past to designing policies which would accelerate the responsiveness of the economy to changing market signals. This is because policy-makers have tended either to have a strong ideological belief that a market economy functions best when there is least intervention by government, or to hold beliefs similarly strongly in centralised intervention through bodies such as the National Enterprise Board and instruments such as planning agreements.

Also when policies have been developed to help industry, they have usually not been informed by any understanding of the need constantly to shift industry towards higher value-added products, or of the changed pattern of production which should emerge if this objective is successfully pursued.

We offer a characterisation of the type of structure of production towards which the economy needs to be moved later in this chapter (pp 33 and 34). If, however, industry is to be encouraged to be more responsive to market signals and resources are to be redeployed more rapidly into the most productive uses, the first requirement is that policy-makers come to understand the powerful new forces that are reshaping world markets, and the reasons why certain companies and countries are successful in them. Currently three factors are of particular importance in terms of the strategies that companies and governments must seek to develop. They are the increasing trend towards global markets, the rise of the Newly Industrialising Countries, and the impact of new technology.

The Trend Towards Global Markets

In a number of important industries and products, competition has taken on a global nature. This means much more than that the market involved is one which is dominated by multinationals. In many markets, multinationals compete on a multi-domestic basis, that is to say they develop different strategies for each of their foreign markets, and look at competition independently from market to market. But in a global industry, the strategic position of multinationals in different foreign markets is critically affected by their overall global position, and they, therefore, develop strategies which take account of their product and market positions worldwide.

Why have more industries and products become global ones in recent years? There are a number of reasons. First, there is the increasing capital-intensity of manufacture. In a growing number of markets there are economies of scale in production or providing a service which extend beyond the size of major national markets. For example, as Honda became a global company in the field of motorcycles, it exploited economies of scale by means of its centralised manufacturing and logistics facilities. The fact that it was selling over 50,000 units per month meant that it was able to use less costly manufacturing techniques than other motorcycle producers with lower volumes.

Secondly, the accelerating pace and scale of R. and D. in many industries means that the company which can recoup these costs by selling the resulting products in a number of markets around the world has a major competitive advantage. Computers, aircraft, and semiconductors are industries where the ability to sell worldwide appears to give a technological advantage. Telecommunications became a global industry when in the 1970's electronic switching technology was introduced, and the initial R. and D. investment required to develop a new system jumped to more than $100 million.

Thirdly, improved communications, including mass travel, have created a significant trend towards world products and services. This is most noticeable in fashionable consumer goods such as Coca Cola, Levi's, McDonalds and pop music, but is increasingly apparent also in consumer durables and capital goods. Finally, the trend towards global markets is dependent on there being methods of transport which are cheap enough to enable the economies of centralised production and development to be passed on to the final customer.

The Rise of the Newly Industrialising Countries

The second factor which has had a major impact on the dynamics of world markets is the increasing role played by the Newly Industrialising Countries (NICs) such as South Korea, Taiwan, Singapore and Brazil. They are now all significant exporters of manufactured goods, and during the 1970's they grew at over 13 per cent per annum. What we are seeing here is the bringing on-stream of productive cheap labour in the Third World.

Because of the growth of literacy which is taking place in the Third World, cheap labour which once could not be used because it was not productive enough, is now starting to reach productivity levels which make it competitive in world markets. And the impact can be very dramatic.

In the case of fibre production, for instance, if UK labour costs are 100, then the index of labour costs in South Korea is 20 (Stopford and Baden Fuller, 1982). Now if the UK labour force was more productive than that of South Korea, it might still be possible for the UK to compete. Unfortunately, in this case the UK is less productive. If we take productivity in the UK as being 100, then the productivity of a South Korean labourer is 113. Put these two figures together and Korea's effective labour cost is 18. In these circumstances, it is easy to become pessimistic about the economic prospects of the UK. If the NICs are able broadly to purchase the same machines as we can, and if they can acquire the same technologies as we can, and if their workers are prepared to accept much lower wages than those in the UK, can we not expect them gradually to climb the technological ladder, leaving this country with only advanced products such as aerospace and advanced information technology? As far as the future of British industry is concerned, this is the key question. Because, if the NICs do progress rapidly up the technological ladder, then the only options open to Britain will be de-industrialisation or protectionism on a massive scale.

In assessing the strength of the challenge from the NICs, however, it is important to be clear both where the current battlefield lies, and what are the factors which will determine the outcome of the battle.

Figure 1 categorises industries by their research intensity.

Figure 1—Industry Research Intensity (Turner, June 1983)

High Tech.	Intermediate	Low Tech.
Aerospace	Chemicals (Indust. and Agric.)	Building materials
Office Equipment		
Computers	Automobiles	Textiles
Electronics and	Industrial and Farm	Leather Goods
Electrical appliances	Equipment	
Pharmaceuticals	Rubber	Paper and Wood
Chemicals (Consum.)		Food
		Tobacco
		Drink

If one then looks at the industries where the NICs have done well, it will be seen that they are the low technology ones. They have so far not got into high technology areas such as office equipment and pharmaceuticals. The battle is currently being fought out in the intermediate areas like automobiles. And what the outcome of this battle will be is not yet clear.

It used to be thought that cars would prove to be the cotton textiles of the next decade and that as a mature industry with a stable, transferable technology and high labour costs the car industry would migrate to the developing countries. But this has not happened on anything like the scale predicted. This is partly due to the transitional inefficiencies and costs that are involved in building up a sufficiently large and sophisticated components industry. It is also because the automobile industry has ceased to be a mature industry with a stable technology which the NICs can easily buy and apply to their industries. After a period of incremental technological change, electronics and new materials are having a major impact on the industry, with the result that management skills are once again a critical resource. Cheap, semi-skilled labour is no longer a decisive advantage.

Recent experience in automobiles may well be replicated elsewhere. In a world of rapidly evolving technologies and short product cycles, management skills may very likely turn out to be more important in many industries than cheap labour. Equally, it may be easier for the Europeans and the Americans to learn from the Japanese than from the NICs, in which case, we may be able to compete in many more industries than is currently thought. It is an elementary mistake to divide industries simply into "sunrise" and "sunset" ones. The new technologies will have applications in many industries: in many industries there will be parts which depend critically on management skills. It is also probable that in many parts of industry, automation will make the level of wages irrelevant.

As John Pinder, the former Director of the Policy Studies Institute, has written:

"It follows from the breadth of the new industrial revolution that the industrial countries should not regard a few high technology sectors as the last bastion in which they can seek refuge. This is the end of the spectrum at which they have the greatest advantage, and they would certainly be foolish not to ensure that they occupy it. But these sectors cannot provide more than a small part of total added-value and employment. It has been a fault of British research policy to give too large a share of resources to nuclear power and aerospace. The health of an economy will depend more on the effectiveness with which the new technologies are applied across the whole range of industrial and service activities. It follows that specialisation should be seen, not as a choice of winning sectors, but as a general function of a progressive economy, in which technological and managerial skills ensure that opportunities are exploited in whatever sector these skills can usefully be applied."

The Impact of Technology

The third factor which it is necessary to examine if we are to understand the dynamics of world markets today, is technology. A number of recent economic studies have made it clear that the competitive performance of nations, industries and companies cannot be explained in terms of traditional price competition theory, but must be explained in terms of their ability to understand and use technology to meet market needs.

A convincing demonstration of the importance of technology in explaining differences in international competitiveness was made by Pavitt and Soete. They regressed US patenting data available for forty industrial branches since 1963 against the value of exports from the OECD countries. In twenty-three of the forty sectors they found a statistically significant relationship. The industries which showed a high statistical correlation included all those which have a high R. and D. intensity. This is not surprising because, of course, these are the industries where R. and D. measures are a reasonably good proxy for the process of innovation. The two areas where non-significant results were obtained were traditional materials such as stone, rubber and concrete, and non-durable consumer goods such as textiles and food products. The explanation for these two areas being different put forward by Pavitt and Soete was that these are the industries where conventional factor endowments such as low wage rates and natural resources play an important role in determining export competitiveness.

Such statistical correlation studies of international trade can be corroborated by studies which have looked at the importance of "non-price factors" in explaining international competitiveness. Rothwell, for example, surveyed in 1977, 107 UK textile companies. They were asked if they bought foreign built textile machinery between 1970 and 1976, and, if so, why. 27 per cent said that a machine to suit their requirements simply did not exist in the UK, while 32 per cent said that the superior overall performance of foreign machines was the reason why they had bought a foreign machine. Only 4 per cent said that they had bought foreign built machinery because it was cheaper.

Technology has a great ability to change the nature of world markets. It is the source of many new products, and new manufacturing technology can lead to mature products being produced more cheaply. Technology also has an enormous power to change the rules of the game. Switzerland used to have a huge share of the world market for watches because of the world lead that Swiss craftsmen had in producing accuracy. But the invention of mass-produced, large-scale, integrated chips and frequency oscillators meant that accuracy could be produced very easily. Their use in watches led to a loss of value-added by the Swiss watch industry. The Swiss are now fighting back with products such as the Swatch, which combines innovative marketing with new technology for bonding the parts of the watch into the case, but this is only after ten years of being battered by the watchmakers of Japan and Hong Kong. As well as nullifying the advantages of incumbents, technology can also change industry boundaries and create new substitute products. The capability to understand and use technology to satisfy market needs is, therefore, a key factor in explaining international competitiveness.

Building Competitive Advantage

These are the major forces reshaping world markets. But what should the answer of British industry be to the competitive challenge that they pose? What strategies should British companies adopt when faced with global markets? Is there any way that British industry can compete against the Newly Industrialising Countries without cutting the real wages of their workers? How can technology be used to increase the value-added per person in industry? In seeking to provide answers to these questions it is necessary to make use of concepts developed to aid corporate strategists. The problems facing particular industries are quite different. Only by using the concepts of corporate strategy can we understand the range of problems that industry faces, and the range of solutions that industry must evaluate. Equally, programmes of support for industry devised by Government will only be effective if they reinforce the competitive strategies of firms within particular industries.

28

A central concept of corporate strategy is that of competitive advantage, because it is the means by which a company is able to outperform its rivals, and, thereby, increase its value-added. There are many different ways of achieving competitive advantage. But as Michael Porter has pointed out there are only two broad types of competitive advantage: lower cost on the one hand and differentiation or uniqueness on the other. Based on these two fundamental sources of competitive advantage, and looking at the range of the company's target market, only three generic competitive strategies can be distinguished.

"Overall cost leadership: the firm seeks industrywide cost leadership in serving a broad range of industry segments.

Overall differentiation: the firm seeks industrywide differentiation in serving a broad range of industry segments.

Focus: the firm directs its entire strategy at a narrow target business segment, foregoing sales to other segments. By tuning the strategy exclusively to the target, it seeks to achieve cost leadership or differentiation or both in serving this narrow target even though it does not achieve these advantages overall."

But how does a company achieve overall cost leadership, overall differentiation, or the advantages of a focused strategy? There are many ways. A company may seek, for example, to gain overall cost leadership by achieving greater scale in its manufacturing operations, or by better product yield, longer run lengths or better manufacturing technology. It may seek to differentiate itself by being faster than its competitors at introducing new products, or it may seek to achieve competitive advantage by focusing on the needs of a small group of customers. The small delicatessen which stays open very late and delivers to its customers' homes, but has very high prices, is adopting a focused strategy.

A classic example of an industry gaining cost leadership by means of lower production costs is the Japanese colour television industry (Magaziner and Hout, 1980). In 1970 production volumes were quite low and the industry only exported 17 per cent of its output. At that time Japanese productivity in television set manufacture was also slightly lower than that in Europe and the USA. But by 1978 the Japanese industry produced over half of non-Comecon colour television sales, and its productivity in set assembly was three to five times greater than that of its world competitors. How was this success achieved at a time when Japanese wages were rising rapidly and the yen appreciating? Mainly by heavy investment linked to major improvements in process and product engineering. In particular three factors contributed significantly to the increase in productivity: a reduced number of components in a set; an increased use of automation in insertion and materials handling; and a reduced number of circuit boards in a set. By 1978 automatic insertion was used for approximately 70 to 80 per cent of all electrical components in a Japanese television set at a time when the average for European producers was only 15 to 30 per cent.

Japanese sets had also become much more reliable than European sets due to a higher level of pre-production component testing, greater automatic testing of insertion, and larger volumes for each chassis design which allowed more "debugging" of each one. Scale was a key factor in achieving these improvements, and by this time the Japanese producers had already overtaken their western competitors both in average factory volume and cumulative volume per chassis type.

By contrast Casio, the Japanese manufacturer of watches and pocket calculators, has followed a strategy of differentiating itself from its competitors by bringing out a stream of new products (Ohmae, 1983). For example, it brought out its 2mm thick card-size calculator, dropped the price to discourage its competitors from producing a similar product, and a few months later produced another model which emits musical notes when the numerical keys are pressed.

Casio is able to produce this stream of new products because it has organised itself in a different way from its competitors. They have maintained the traditional divisions between engineering, manufacturing and marketing, and they have also integrated vertically by owning their own integrated circuitry production facilities. Casio has, however, remained an engineering, marketing and assembly company, and has integrated its design and development functions into marketing so that consumers' needs and desires are analysed by those closest to the market and quickly turned into new products.

For an example of a company with a focused strategy it is necessary to look no further than ICL, the largest British-owned computer company. For many years ICL tried to compete head-on with IBM in the globally competitive computer market, in spite of the fact that with sales of £1bn it is one-fiftieth of the size of IBM. It managed to survive because of the protection afforded it by the UK public sector, but in 1982 was close to the brink of bankruptcy. As a result a new management team was brought in who quickly developed a new strategy.

Instead of seeking to produce better mainframe computers than IBM, an impossible task given the size of the two companies, ICL has recently with some success sought to focus tightly on selling specialised systems to narrow market segments where it can achieve leadership. It has, for example, sought to develop a strong position in certain niche markets such as retailing, manufacturing, and financial services. Also, instead of trying to develop everything itself, and span virtually the whole market, it has been prepared to buy in products and technology from Japan and elsewhere, or develop them collaboratively. As a result it has managed to survive and prosper in an industry which is dominated by industrial giants.

It can be seen then that strategies can be developed which enable companies to adapt to the changing dynamics of world markets without cutting back the real wages of their workers or seeking protectionism. The case studies illustrate that, to be successful, companies in the modern world need constantly to shift the pattern of their production towards higher value-added products. Different types of strategy are appropriate in different circumstances, but all require management skills of a high order. Few firms are likely to be able to compete successfully in world markets solely on the basis of price.

The Restructuring of British Industry

We need in Britain to follow the example of the Japanese who have for a long time understood the need constantly to restructure industry towards higher value-added or "knowledge-intensive" industries, or parts of industries, if a country's standard of living is to rise in a sustained way. This belief shared by civil servants and businessmen has been one of the constant themes of Japanese industrial policy and is well illustrated by a speech by Mr. Y. Ojimi, Vice Minister of International Trade and Industry, to the OECD Industrial Committee in Tokyo on 24th June, 1970 (Magaziner and Hout, 1980)

> "Industrialisation in developing countries will stimulate competitive relations in the markets of advanced nations in products with a low degree of processing. As a result, the confrontation between free trade and protectionism will become more intense.
>
> The solution of this problem is to be found according to economic logic, in progressively giving away industries to other countries much as a big brother gives his out-grown clothes to his younger brother. In this way, a country's own industries become more sophisticated.
>
> A solution of the North–South problem depends not only on internal development for developing nations, but also on giving them fair opportunities in the area of trade.
>
> To do this, the advanced nations must plan for sophistication of their industrial structures and open their market for unsophisticated merchandise as well as offer aid in the form of funds and technology."

The Japanese approach can also be illustrated by Diagram I taken from a report of the Japanese Economic Planning Agency in 1974–75 (Magaziner and Hout, 1980). The changing contours of the diamond show how Japan's exports at different times have split between four different types of industry which have different requirements for success. In 1959 Japan's export mix was mainly skewed towards unskilled labour intensive products such as clothing, footwear and toys. In the 1960's and 1970's, however, it shifted towards more capital intensive products such as steel, motor cycles and ships. The diamond also illustrates how the Japanese Economic Planning Agency hoped that Japan would have by 1985 a mix of exports with a high proportion in knowledge-intensive areas such as computers and medical instruments.

DIAGRAM I
EVOLUTION OF INDUSTRIAL STRUCTURE
JAPAN

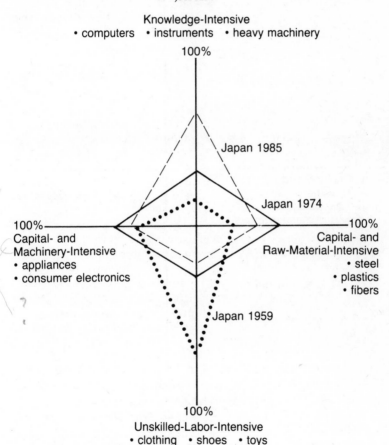

Source: Japanese Economic Planning Agency

It is instructive to compare the rapid evolution of Japan's economic structure with the evolution of Britain's. This is

DIAGRAM II
EVOLUTION OF INDUSTRIAL STRUCTURE
UK

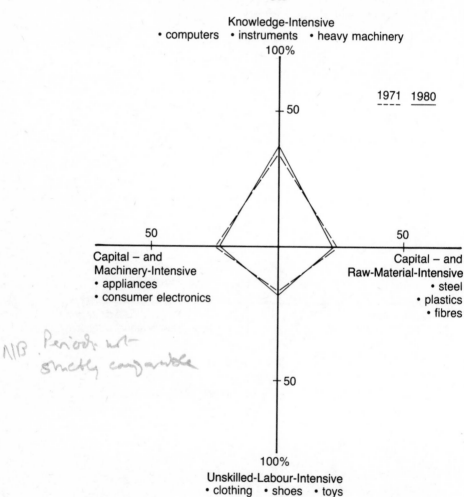

Knowledge-Intensive
• computers   • instruments   • heavy machinery
100%

1971 1980

50

50   50

Capital – and   Capital – and
Machinery-Intensive   Raw-Material-Intensive
• appliances   • steel
• consumer electronics   • plastics
                                                      • fibres

NB. Periods not
strictly comparable

50

100%
Unskilled-Labour-Intensive
• clothing   • shoes   • toys

illustrated in Diagram II, which shows that in the course of the
1970's Britain's pattern of production adapted hardly at all in
face of the rapid developments in world markets. The allocation
of resources between different types of activity was apparently
"fossilised".

34

Instead of debating how we can compete against low-wage countries by holding wages back, in Britain we need to follow the example of Japan and devote more of our efforts towards restructuring industry towards more knowledge-intensive activities. Raising the level of value-added per person in British industry presents of course a formidable challenge. But a determined and constructive drive to help industry restructure to meet the demands of the markets of the future is more likely to deliver the goods in terms of future prosperity than the current approach to improving "competitiveness". This simply involves holding back increases in living standards. It amounts to acquiescence in industrial decline.

A Strategic Role for Government

We have seen that there is a constant need for a country to restructure industry, and to seek higher levels of value-added per person, but what is the role of government in this process? The evidence from the most successful economies in the world suggests that the government cannot leave everything to the market. To compete in global markets today a country must organise itself to win. If it does not do so, it will be beaten by those that do.

In the world of traditional economics no account is taken of social organisation and institution building, and the government can leave everything to the market. A country is endowed with its comparative advantage and should specialise in those products which use intensively the factors of production found locally in abundance. If it has a lot of labour relative to capital, it should export labour intensive products, and if it has a lot of capital relative to labour, it should export capital intensive products. The theory also assumes diminishing marginal returns and a law of increasing costs, full employment, costless factor mobility and universal access to production technologies. But economic reality differs in fundamental respects from this type of approach.

In the first place, technological knowledge in the form of equipment, know-how and patents is not available to all-comers. It is, in fact, jealously guarded by companies because it gives them a competitive advantage. A second weakness of the theory is its belief in a law of rising costs. This may hold in the short-term, but there is now plenty of evidence to show that, particularly in high technology industries, long run costs decline in real terms, partly from economies of scale and partly because of learning curves. As a result the high volume producers are also usually the low cost producers. Finally, the traditional view is a static one, where efficiency is achieved by getting to a fixed production frontier, whereas in the real world a great deal of time and money is expended in moving the production frontier outward by means of R. and D. expenditure and other improvements in efficiency.

In the real world, comparative advantage can be created as well as simply inherited, as has been shown both in America and Japan. Furthermore, in this process of creating comparative advantage government can play an important strategic role. Because of the success of American agriculture since the last war it is easy to fall into the trap of believing that it has always been highly productive due to having been blessed with good soil, a good climate and highly motivated farmers (Thurow, 1985). But in the 1930's American agriculture was a very sick industry, and its productivity was well below the rest of the economy. American agriculture became a success story because of a strategy, started in the 1930's, which shifted it from being a low technology industry to being a high technology one, and which depended heavily on government funds. Large amounts of money were put into agricultural research at state agricultural colleges. The results of this research were further developed at state experimental farms, and then spread to individual farmers by country agents. Major investments were also made to improve the physical infrastructure, and the Rural Electrification Administration was set up to bring electricity to every farm in America. America built up its comparative advantage in agriculture. It did not simply inherit it. Present day problems of agricultural over-production on a world wide scale do not diminish that historical achievement.

Similarly it is important to understand that Japan's remarkable post-war economic growth was based on a rejection of a static theory of comparative advantage. After the war, the Governor of the Bank of Japan advocated policies based on existing characteristics of the Japanese economy—a huge supply of under-employed labour, an extreme scarcity of capital and out-of-date technology. In terms of a static theory of comparative advantage this implied that support should be given to labour-intensive industries such as textiles, clothing and pottery. But after a major debate Japanese leaders, advised by the Ministry of International Trade and Industry (MITI), rejected such a development strategy, and gave support instead to industries which required the intensive use of capital and technology such as steel, petrochemicals and automobiles. In reality they had decided upon a strategy of dynamic comparative advantage (Shinohara, 1982). The two criteria they used to select industries were an "income elasticity criterion" and a "comparative technical progress criterion". According to the "income elasticity criterion" industries were to be supported whose elasticity of export demand with respect to world real income as a whole was comparatively high. The "comparative technical progress criterion" suggested support for industries which can more rapidly gain comparative advantage by the input of technical knowledge. In this way Japan showed that it is possible deliberately to upgrade the comparative advantage of a country. Again, Britain has a lot to learn from the Japanese in building competitive advantage.

It is clear that in countries like Japan the government has played a key role in upgrading the industrial structure of the country. If value-added per person in British industry is to be substantially increased government will also have to play an important strategic role. The thrust of policy should be to help accelerate the movement of resources into knowledge-intensive industries. This will involve both a change of priorities for government and also a new definition of what it is expected to do.

The task of upgrading Britain's industrial structure is a massive one. It will require not only a major improvement in the performance of British managers but also significant changes in, for example, education, the deployment of R. and D. resources and the tax system, all of which will raise industry's capacity to compete in the markets of the future. In all these areas there are vested interests and inertia. The necessary changes will only take place if the government is determined to give priority to the needs of industry. There will be people who will argue against such a change on the grounds that either it is not necessary or that society has more important values. But, if as a country we are seriously concerned about inner city decay, poverty and high unemployment, we must give priority to improving our industrial performance.

We need also to define clearly the strategic role that we want government to play. In the past British political parties have tended to believe that all intervention by government is good or that all intervention is harmful. By contrast experience in other countries would suggest that there are some policy areas where government can make a significant contribution, whilst in others government is likely to do more harm than good.

There are two main ways in which government can help industry. First, the government should seek to improve the performance of British industry by creating a dynamic and competitive environment for it. In this way resources will flow more quickly into the knowledge-intensive parts of industry best able to compete in world markets.

If industry is protected from foreign or domestic competition, and if opportunities are not taken to expose monopolies to competition wherever possible, then no one should be surprised if industry is slow to react to new competitive opportunities or threats. Competition requires hard work and sacrifice, and companies that don't have to compete in all probability will not. Protection is usually sold by politicians on the grounds that an industry needs time to restructure and develop new products, but it is difficult to think of an established industry which having been given protection has become a world-class competitor again.

A competitive market economy is also the best way, we believe, to decentralise industrial decision-making and to prevent government ministers from being overburdened with decisions which they are not competent to take. In the past Labour politicians have become heavily involved in particular industrial decisions, which at the most have probably affected no more than 5 per cent of the economy, while adopting other policies which hindered efficiency and the re-allocation of resources. As a result the net effect of government policy has been harmful. In Chapter 3 we set out the detailed policies we would like to see the government adopt to create a more dynamic and competitive environment for industry.

Secondly, we believe that government has an important strategic role to play in making certain that industry has the necessary resources to compete with foreign companies. If the education and training of managers and the workforce is significantly below that of our competitors, or the technological infrastructure is worse, or the cost of capital is higher, this will put industry at a serious disadvantage in world markets. In many cases general measures will be appropriate, aimed at raising the performance of industry across the board, but the government should also be sufficiently close to industry to help particular industries in specific ways, especially those developing knowledge-intensive activities. Co-operative R. and D. arrangements and rationalisation cartels are obvious areas where government can give help to particular industries. But it should also seek to aid industries in other ways, such as, for example, making certain that the provision of roads and airports takes into account the needs of tourism, and that the regulation of the City enhances its reputation as an international financial centre.

It will be argued by some people, of course, that government policies have not ignored the needs of industry. Is not the British businessman or Trade Unionist, depending on one's political prejudices, the real villain? The answer is that short-term social and military objectives have to an extraordinary extent been allowed to take precedence over industrial needs. If we look at education and training, or the allocation of technological resources, or the financial markets, in almost all cases the needs of industry have been given a low priority. In Chapter 4 we will look at some fundamental changes which need to be made in these areas.

Finally, it follows from all that has been said above that the aim of the government's industrial policies should not be to substitute government direction for market signals, but to speed up the process of adjustment by companies. Resources need to be moved into those segments of an industry which depend for their success on a higher level of skills, such as high fashion textiles, and also into those industries which are more knowledge-intensive. This means that all government policies for industry should be judged against the basic criterion of whether or not they speed up the process of change.

CHAPTER 3

Making Markets Work Better

Technology, costs and markets are changing today with increasing rapidity: if companies are to survive they must adapt equally fast. The success of Japanese industry, for example, can be explained to a great extent by the speed with which Japanese companies respond to change. This speed of response can in turn be largely attributed to the intense rivalry which exists between large Japanese industrial groups and which takes the form of far-reaching price competition, investment "races", and "doubling strategies" by which capacity and output are doubled in two or four years.

By contrast, study after study has shown that British companies seek to avoid competition and are slow to innovate, while new technologies diffuse slowly in the British economy. This slowness cannot be attributed simply to the malign influence of the Trade Unions or management. For every company that goes into liquidation because of restrictive work practices another collapses because its management has failed to develop new products. A reluctance to change is a feature of our society, and is not restricted to any single group.

A key question, therefore, which any government must ask is whether the dynamism and competitive behaviour of industry can be improved by competition policy. We believe that it can. Competition policy and trade policy must be at the centre of any effective policy for industry, and not peripheral issues as they have often been in the past.

In particular there are three key areas where the government needs to have a clear and consistent view. First, the government

41

must have a firm competition policy which prevents companies from sharing out markets, creating monopolies or adopting predatory pricing policies to bankrupt small businesses. Secondly, the government must make certain that statutory monopolies are opened up to competition as far as possible. This is far more important than the linked but separate question of ownership of their assets, which has dominated the last forty years of British politics with disastrous results. Finally, the government must seek to protect British interests abroad while not yielding to the temptation to shield British industry from foreign competition.

Competition at Home

British industry has not welcomed rivalry between firms, while Government policy has done little to expose it to more competition. It is difficult to estimate the degree of rivalry among companies, but a rough indication can be got by looking at firms' pricing behaviour, in particular the extent to which prices change as costs and levels of demand change. Recent research in this area shows that in Japan prices are very flexible both absolutely and in relation to price behaviour elsewhere in the OECD, while price flexibility in the UK is at the other end of the spectrum (Ergas, 1984). Price flexibility is particularly low in the more concentrated industries in the UK. The evidence also suggests that the US, Sweden and West Germany lie somewhere between these two extremes.

This lack of rivalry between British businessmen is not, however, surprising. During the 1930's, British industry, as part of the trend towards protectionism, became heavily cartelised, often with the explicit support of government departments. These cartels in manufacturing industry in the mid-1950's were estimated to cover some 50–60 per cent of output, and it was only with the Restrictive Practices Act of 1956 that a presumption that they were against the public interest was embodied in the law.

Moreover, in spite of a number of major pieces of legislation, successive governments have not constructed effective machinery for enforcing competition. Actions which reduce competition are not automatically regarded as harmful, and a public interest test is applied on a case-by-case basis. Sanctions are few so that if a company believes that it can increase its profits by restricting competition, it is probably in its financial interest to do so. And, finally, the machinery for enforcing competition is very bureaucratic and far too complicated.

There are essentially three organisations involved. The Monopolies and Mergers Commissions (MMC) has no powers of initiative. The Secretary of State for Trade and Industry is responsible for referring mergers to it. Before a merger can be referred to the Commission, the assets involved must exceed £30 million or the merger must create or strengthen a market share of at least 25 per cent.

The Director General of Fair Trading is responsible for overseeing consumer affairs and competition policy. Where monopolies are concerned, he can make references on his own intitiative to the MMC, but in the case of mergers his role is to advise the Secretary of State for Trade and Industry. The MMC is also not asked to approve mergers or monopolies. It is asked simply to investigate and report on whether the monopoly or merger "operates, or may be expected to operate, against the public interest."

Then there is the Restrictive Practices Court which deals with such practices as price-fixing or market sharing agreements by companies. Agreements are referred to it by the Director General of Fair Trading. This Court has been very successful in a limited area. As a result of its actions overt cartels and resale price maintenance have been almost totally outlawed. Unfortunately, such practices have all too often been replaced by underhand cartels and indirect ways of enforcing resale price maintenance.

A further dimension to competition policy is provided by European Community competition law and its associated enforcement machinery. Articles 85 and 86 of the 1957 Treaty of Rome govern European Community competition where trade between member states is concerned, and are directly enforceable in British courts. Article 85 of the Treaty covers agreements and connected practices in restraint of trade, which is essentially the same ground as covered by the Restrictive Trade Practices Act. Article 86 covers abuses of monopoly or dominant positions such as predatory pricing, which is basically the ground covered by the 1980 Competition Act.

This complicated machinery has been ineffective in two major ways. First, it has not been very successful in promoting greater competition. It has effectively put an end to overt price-fixing agreements as well as large horizontal mergers since the 1970's but otherwise its impact has not been great. Primarily this is because its effectiveness is limited almost entirely to the particular cases which it decides to examine. In the United States, by contrast, enforcement is not restricted to the acceptance of cases by a bureaucracy. The courts award damages against firms found guilty of anti-competitive practices, and consequently a body of case law has grown up which has a deterrent effect much wider than the particular cases considered.

Secondly the current machinery for enforcing competition has done very little to stem the recent rapid acceleration in merger and acquisition activity. The scale of mergers and takeovers in recent years has been huge. In 1981 it was £1.1 billion. By 1984 it had risen to £5.3 billion, rising further to nearly £7 billion in 1985, and it had already reached £10.5 billion by the third quarter of 1986. The 1985 figure of £7 billion is equivalent to half the amount of expenditure on plant and machinery in Britain in that year.

The argument against this merger and acquisition activity is not, however, that it absorbs funds, and thereby starves the economy of investment. When Hanson Trust takes over Imperial Foods it borrows money to pay the shareholders of Imperial Foods, who then return the money to the financial markets. Rather merger and acquisition activity on the scale that we have experienced shortens the time horizons of management and distracts them from the more important task of building up competitive advantage by means of new products, processes and distribution channels. Management's time horizons are inevitably shortened because to take over other companies (or defend oneself from being taken over) ever-rising profits and a high P/E (price/earnings) multiple are necessary. This makes companies reluctant to undertake long-term investment which may build up competitive advantage, but which may temporarily depress profits and make them vulnerable to a takeover. The endless rearranging of the ownership of assets also signals to top management that the way to get rich quick, and expand their companies, is by a well-timed takeover rather than the hard and lengthy process of improving the efficiency of their companies.

What action then should government take to improve the level of competition between British companies? There is a need both to simplify the machinery for implementing competition policy, and to strengthen the policy itself. A first step is to merge the three organisations that currently exist into one body, a new Office of Fair Trading, with the courts providing recourse for cases brought by individuals and companies independently of it, or after it has determined a case. The new body should be vested with executive authority comparable to that exercised by the Federal Trade Commission in the United States and the European Commission. As with all statutory bodies it should be answerable to the courts.

But as well as new machinery competition policy should itself be strengthened in two important ways. At present, for a monopoly or merger to be stopped, it is necessary to show that it ". . . operates, or may be expected to operate, against the public interest." Even when the benefits of a merger seem non-existent, it is often difficult to show that it actually operates against the public interest. Instead of a presumption in favour of mergers, there should be a presumption against them unless it can be shown that positive economic benefits will flow from the joining together of the two companies concerned. In assessing whether mergers should go ahead, the two main criteria should be whether the merger would lead to greater wealth creation, and whether it would lead to an increased ability to compete in world markets. Shifting the onus of proof in this way would not stop takeovers where managers have demonstrably failed, or where real benefits can be achieved. But it should dampen down the level of mergers and acquisitions which have no economic logic.

Additionally individuals and companies should be given the right to initiate actions in the courts, and to be awarded damages where anti-competitive behaviour has been established. The current arrangement whereby the Director of Fair Trading has the power to investigate and seek voluntary agreement from firms to change their practices has considerable merit. But new legal rights for individuals and companies to initiate actions, and to be awarded damages, would act as a much more effective deterrent, as well as having more of an impact on the economy as a whole.

However, while there is a strong case for trying to increase the level of rivalry between British companies, it is very important that this does not lead to any reductions in areas of legitimate co-operation such as research and development (R. and D.). As a result both of the growth of global competition that we have outlined as well as limited resources, it is now clear that many companies are not in a position to follow a "go-it-alone" R. and D. strategy (Fusfeld and Haklisch, 1985). In Japan, this has led to such co-operative efforts as the four-year Very Large Scale Integration programme (VLSI) and the ten-year Fifth Generation Computer Systems programme. At first the Americans were slow to respond to this threat. Recently, however, there has been a growth of research corporations such as the Microelectronics and Computer Technology Corporation and the Semiconductor Research Corporation. In Europe the Esprit programme has been launched. These are all legitimate ways of cutting the costs of technological development, and of increasing the speed with which new technologies are diffused in the economy. Competition policy should facilitate this type of co-operation, not discourage it.

In some circumstances there may also be a case for permitting agreements between companies to reduce excess capacity. The marketplace can, of course, be allowed to achieve the same result, but there are problems in letting it do so. The companies which survive will not necessarily be the most efficient ones, but those that start with the most financial resources. Moreover the long period of losses necessary to drive the weakest companies out of business may fatally weaken the surviving ones. In Japan, to deal with these situations, their Parliament passed in May 1978, the Structurally Depressed Industries Law (Magaziner and Reich, 1982). This enables MITI to develop stabilisation plans for depressed industries using government funds. A government loan guarantee fund aids producers to scrap or mothball capacity. Industries only become eligible for assistance, however, if two-thirds of the producers petition

MITI, which then has discretion over whether to grant their request. This condition enables MITI to get agreement among producers whose solutions are likely to be very different. But as the Lazard Scheme for U.K. steel castings showed such rationalisation schemes have to be managed very carefully if they are to lead to an improvement in the workings of the market (Baden Fuller and Hill, 1984).

Liberalisation, Privatisation and Regulation

The ownership of key strategic industries, particularly the public utilities, has been a major area of debate in British politics since the war. Nationalisation and privatisation have been inflicted on certain industries with an almost total lack of concern for their long-term efficiency. At the same time very little attention has been given to the more important question of how they can be exposed to greater competition, even though the limited evidence available suggests that this is a more effective way to improve their performance. A government committed to improving the efficiency of British industry should, therefore, switch its attention away from poorly-conceived and hastily executed changes in the ownership of industries to a long-term programme of liberalisation.

A clear example of the impact liberalisation can have is the change that took place in express coaching after a significant deregulation was introduced in 1980. Major improvements took place in output, fares and the quality and range of services provided. The performance of British Telecom in the City has also dramatically improved, because that is where competition from Mercury has produced a real threat.

There is equally much merit in the privatisation in recent years of companies such as Jaguar and the National Freight Corporation which were already operating in a competitive environment. On the other hand the benefits of privatisation where there is little or no competition are not so clear. Studies comparing the performance of the public and private sectors do not unambiguously show that the private sector will always do better than the public sector. Three industries have been studied in detail, the airlines, ferries and hovercraft, and the sale of electricity and gas appliances: the evidence there suggests that the private sector performs better. But these studies necessarily take place in industries where there is competition. It is likely that where competition exists it will act as more of an incentive to the private sector than to the public sector. It is not so obvious that private sector monopolies which are subject to regulation will perform better than public monopolies. In neither case is there the spur of competition, while regulation brings its own distortions of performance.

It is not difficult to see why this is so if we look at the incentives which the managements of such organisations face. A large monopoly such as British Gas which is transferred to the private sector is in reality under very little pressure to improve its performance. Raising money from the capital markets will never cause much of a problem unless its profitability falls drastically. Its size means that it will not be vulnerable to a takeover even if management performs very badly. It will, however, suffer from the inefficiency which regulation can bring. In the United States the problem of "regulatory capture", whereby the regulatory agency comes to identify with the interests of the companies it is supposed to regulate, is regarded as significant. There is also the major problem of how to control prices without giving incentives to companies to be inefficient. If, for example, prices are set on the basis of a maximum rate of return on assets, companies have very little incentive to be efficient, as costs can be passed on in prices, and there is the real danger that companies will over-invest.

Governments in future should, therefore, seek to get away from the ideological debate between public and private ownership. Instead they should focus on ways of increasing competition and giving better incentives to public monopolies. The scope for doing so will, of course, vary from industry to industry. For example, when the present government privatised British Gas, no new competition was introduced despite clear opportunities to do so.

But British Gas could have been restructured. One company could have been given the task of operating the National Transmission System, which transmits the gas from the beachhead landing-points to the different regions of the country, with an obligation to carry gas produced from any source on non-discriminatory terms. The twelve regions could have become twelve independent companies. At the same time the ownership of the existing contracts for the supply of gas on very favourable terms from the oil companies could have been hived off. (These date back in some cases to the 1960's, owe nothing to the foresight of British Gas, and enable it to undercut potential competitors.) This restructuring would have enabled potential entrants to the gas supply market to have competed to supply gas to the regional distributors on a fair basis.

In the case of the water industry, on the other hand, it is very difficult to see how serious competition could be introduced. The local supply of water is a natural monopoly, and the wholesale supply very nearly so. Sewage collection is also a natural monopoly, though this is less true of treatment and disposal. There is no reason to believe that efficiency or customer service would benefit from the transfer of this industry from the public to the private sector. Serious issues of public accountability would also be involved in any such change.

Alongside its policies for encouraging rivalry between domestic companies, the government needs, therefore, to have policies to expose monopoly industries, where possible, to more competition. In many cases these industries are "sheltered industries" which cannot export their products, and are not exposed to foreign competitors. But many provide essential services to British industry. Improvement in their performance must be a major objective of the government.

Free Trade and Protectionism

Active encouragement of rivalry between domestic companies needs to be matched by a commitment not to protect British companies from foreign competition. This is particularly important at the present time because the post-war trend towards a more liberal trading order has now been reversed. In the period between the Bretton Woods Agreement in 1944 and the early 1970's quantitative restrictions on imports of manufactured goods were largely removed. At the same time tariffs were progressively reduced to a very low level. But during the last fifteen years this trend has been reversed through the growth of a range of new restrictive devices. In the world's market economies the share of trade subject to control and restrictions of a non-tariff nature rose on one estimate from 40 per cent to 48 per cent in the years between 1974 and 1980 alone.

This new wave of protectionism has taken a number of forms. Three are of particular importance. First, there is the control of textile and clothing imports from 25 developing countries which is exercised by means of the Multi-Fibre Arrangement. Secondly, there is restricted public purchasing and, finally, and increasingly, there has been the use of "voluntary export restraint agreements". These have proved an extremely convenient device for governments, as they enable them to uphold the principles of free trade in theory while getting around them in practice. Because "voluntary export restraint agreements" are also largely invisible, citizens cannot easily hold their leaders responsible for the substantial costs that these restrictions impose on them.

A whole range of products from Japan to the European Community, including cars, light commercial vehicles, video tape recorders and quartz watches, are now covered by such agreements. These new restrictive devices share many of the obvious disadvantages of unilateral tariffs and quotas.

They free the protected industry from having to improve its performance up to the level of international best practice. They impose additional costs on the consumer. They invite retaliation from our trading partners, and they have an impact on the efficiency of the rest of the economy. Lastly, and most significantly in terms of the argument in Chapter 2, they encourage foreign manufacturers to upgrade their products in order to maintain their earnings, and in that way push them into the high value-added end of the market.

For example, the recent U.S.–Japanese semiconductor trade pact, sought to protect the U.S. semiconductor industry by effectively setting price floors for computer memory chips in the U.S. Predictably it produced howls of protest from chip users who saw their own competitiveness being eroded. It also ensured that the Japanese would be able to make enormous windfall profits on chips. These they are likely to put into developing semicustom chips, the main market where U.S. chip producers have sought refuge from the Japanese. By seeking to shelter their chipmakers without making them more competitive, the U.S. is in danger of losing the ability to supply its high-tech industries with what the Japanese aptly call "industrial rice". The lesson for this country is clear. In co-operation with our trading partners we must seek to resist the rising tide of protectionism, as it will not help us to improve the competitiveness of our products in world markets.

Despite this it would be naive to imagine that "declining industries" will not pressurise governments to give them a period of protection. Governments should resist those pressures. In most cases a better strategy will be to ease the adjustment of capital and labour out of these industries by helping workers with retraining and relocation, by subsidising the development of new businesses within the same region, and by assisting firms to save those parts of their business which are capable of competing in world markets. Sometimes the decline of an industry is so fast, or the impact that its decline will have on a region is so great that the pressures of protectionism may prove irresistible. But protectionism by itself is never the answer. It should always be temporary, and it should always be combined with explicit *quid pro quo*s as to what the industry will do to restore itself to health. By itself protectionism is always a losing strategy.

A case is often made for protectionism for "infant industries". The argument is that an industry may have the potential to compete in world markets, but because its competitors in other countries are further advanced, it needs a period of protection until it is sufficiently large to compete on an international scale. Nevertheless protectionism in these cases can do grave harm to other industries. If one takes the obvious candidates in Britain today such as semiconductors, robotics or personal computers, it is not difficult to see the damage that would be done to other industries if they were given protection. Here again a better strategy for the government in most cases will be to provide funds for research and development, to use public procurement to help the industry by buying advanced products, and to support overseas marketing.

51

The European Dimension

Alongside policies to increase competition among firms at home and maintain free trade, Britain needs to commit itself wholeheartedly to making the European Community into a true common market. American and Japanese companies are given an enormous advantage when it comes to attacking world markets by the large size of their domestic markets. Potentially the European Community offers European companies a similar advantage. In 1984 the United States accounted for 44 per cent of OECD GDP, the European Community for 29 per cent (including Spain and Portugal) and Japan for 15 per cent. Unfortunately, the European Community is not yet a unified market area. Technical barriers to trade within the Community have not been removed. These, together with discriminatory testing and certification procedures, amount effectively to an 8 per cent to 12 per cent tariff. Then there are administrative barriers to trade. The Commission estimates that border delays alone cost traders between 5 per cent and 10 per cent of the value of goods moved. Finally, the procurement policies of European governments continue to discriminate against each other, which according to one estimate may involve purchases equivalent to 17 per cent of GDP.

In a world where a market segment becoming global is often signalled by three or four Japanese companies targeting to achieve 5 per cent world market shares each, it makes no sense for civil servants in European countries to go on backing national champions with a 1 per cent–2 per cent market share who are kept out of other European countries by restrictive public purchasing. Too small to fund the necessary investment to maintain their competitive positions, such national champions have inevitably to rely on significant government support.

As Dr. Rob Wilmot, the former Managing Director and Chief Executive of ICL, has written:

"It is instructive to compare Japan and Europe in VLSI semiconductors. In the early 70's, four Japanese companies (NEC, Hitachi, Fujitsu, Toshiba) set off to achieve 5% world market share. They were sponsored with government research funds and by significant NTT procurement of leading edge product. They achieved economy of scale through massive volumes in consumer electronic products. All achieved 5% world share in the early 80's and were immediately joined by four new companies targeting 5% in the mid 90's (Matsushita, Mitsubishi, Sharp, Oki) and more recently by three more players (Ricoh, Sony, NMB) with similar ambitions for the late 90's.

In contrast, in Europe, the U.K. alone has 5 VLSI semiconductor companies with less than 1% market share. Sweden, Austria, Holland and Italy are already players, with Belgium and Spain about to join the fray."

So what is to be done? To quote from Dr. Wilmot again:

"Clearly, there is a need for a strategy to cope with this dilemma and it *cannot* be a national strategy. It must involve the creation of globally competitive European enterprises with an organisation capability to target the U.S. and Japan. It cannot be based on the very boundaries that are evaporating in the global economy. It must generate wealth in Europe—and will require action by governments working as a team rather than competitors."

The first step that the government must take is to give its vigorous support to the current initiative of the Commission to remove by 1992 all the remaining national barriers to internal trade, including the harmonisation of industrial standards. It is vital that the European Community collaborates over technical standards. The surest way to prevent a European supplier of telecommunications equipment emerging to challenge those of America and Japan is to adopt different technical standards for telecommunications equipment across Europe in order to protect national champions. A significant factor in the success of the Japanese has been their commitment to developing joint standards.

Secondly, we need to create an environment in Europe which encourages the growth of globally competitive European enterprises with the capability to penetrate the markets of the United States and Japan. This should include legislation allowing European incorporation, and could include equalised tax treatment of founder's equity, or options, across the European community in order to encourage start-ups.

Thirdly, European-level initiatives are needed to promote research and development at the pre-competitive stage. The impetus behind research programmes such as ESPRIT, RACE and BRITE should, therefore, be maintained. This pooling of resources is a way to help European industry match the scale of research programmes undertaken in the United States and Japan.

Finally, in both Britain and the European Community we need to take a more balanced view of inward investment. The present Government has encouraged it at every opportunity, while most European governments have fought to see who can give most subsidies to cash-rich American and Japanese companies which are already operating on an international scale. The main criticism of these policies is that because no attempt is made to assess the value of projects, encouragement can be given to those which have little value to the economy and even to those which are actually harmful. An attempt must be made to calculate the long-term *net* addition of such projects to national output. This can be measured roughly by the wages, salaries and taxes the project creates. But in making such calculations it is necessary also to take account of the loss of wages, salaries, profits and taxes elsewhere as a result of the project. A project which replaces existing production with goods which have a higher import content can lead to a net loss rather than a net gain.

This point is of particular importance in the case of high technology firms, where encouraging foreign firms to invest in Britain or Europe may inhibit indigenous companies from achieving the experience and scale economies they require to compete globally. The gains from the unrestricted flow of investment are due to the opportunities it creates for maximising collaboration between resources and expertise in different countries, and we should not seek to hinder such flows. But equally we should be very careful and selective in encouraging them. Some may lead to long term competitive advantage, but some may lead only to a few illusory jobs (Brech and Sharp, 1984).

Free Trade, Competition and Industrial Policies

At the centre of any effective policy for industry must be policies to encourage competition and free trade. Clearly such policies are in conflict with subsidies to "lame ducks", and attempts to slow down market forces. But they are not incompatible with industrial policies to speed up responses to market forces by methods such as raising the standard of education and training, targeting technological resources, or improving the working of financial markets.

Trade wars and protectionism are less likely if policies of this type are adopted. First, if countries have explicit policies to accelerate market forces and ease any necessary hardship, they are less likely to give in to the pressure of interest groups clamouring for protectionism.

Secondly, if a country adopts policies which lead to greater productivity, the growth of new industries, and the easing of labour and capital out of declining industries, then the world economy benefits. It is only when countries adopt policies to retard market forces by protecting declining industries from foreign competition, or by keeping them alive with subsidies, that world trade suffers. The challenge for those responsible for international co-operation, therefore, is to develop rules that encourage wealth creation while adopting rules that ban policies which slow down market forces.

CHAPTER 4

Industrial Policies and Competitive Advantage

While industry needs to be exposed to a competitive climate, it must also have available to it the resources with which to compete. This is a matter of social organisation. If the structure of British industrial production is to adapt towards the high value-added, knowledge-intensive activities which are at the leading edge of economic development—as illustrated by the diamond diagrams in Chapter 2—then our system of education and training, the targeting of our technological resources, and the working of our financial markets must be upgraded and improved to ensure that our industry is in a position to compete at least on equal terms. This will not happen spontaneously but will require a deliberate political initiative, sustained over many years.

We must not, however, make the mistake of thinking that the way to improve performance in these areas is simply to pour in huge sums of additional money. In some key areas extra funds are required. But large aggregate amounts of capital, research and development, or government expenditure will not guarantee success. Competitive advantage depends on how such inputs are used. This means that the government's industrial policies must be market-driven, and judged against the criterion of whether or not they speed up the process of industrial change.

How can industrial policies be tested against the market? In different areas different methods should be used. For example, government should normally only support research projects if industry is itself prepared to put up a significant proportion of the funds. Equally, government can systematically steer funds towards those educational establishments which can show that more of their students are providing industry with the skills they need, or have won more research contracts from industry. If government wants to encourage some particular kind of investment in industry, it should do so by giving a tax credit, such as the Business Expansion Scheme, or by supporting a new kind of financial market, such as the Unlisted Securities Market, rather than by substituting its own judgement for that of industry. If industrial policies are not market-driven, then there is a real danger that they are used to slow down the process of industrial change and prop up companies which are not viable.

Everyone is aware today of the supply-side deficiencies of British industry, but very different views are held about how the government can aid companies to improve the value and quality of the products they produce. Many right-wing economists stress increasing entrepreneurial incentives, removing restraints on the operation of free markets and lightening the burden of government regulations. These are important areas. While much has been done in recent years to improve the situation in this country, more could still be done. For example, there is still plenty of scope to reform the tax and benefit system so that it provides more effective incentives for hard work and entrepreneurial risk-taking at all levels of income. Housing policies are required which make it easier for people to move around the country. And the government must fight an endless battle to see that small businesses are not stifled by red tape.

But more positive measures are also needed to help industry build up competitive advantage. For a company to be successful today in world markets, it cannot afford to be burdened by overmanning or restrictive practices. New methods and technology must be accepted enthusiastically. But these are necessary and not sufficient conditions for success.

Success requires a well-educated and well trained workforce, the organisational capability to use new technologies and produce new products quickly, and the resources to update factories and equipment. Companies must also have a workforce which is committed to its objectives. And what is true for individual companies is also true for industry as a whole. Flexibility is not the only requirement for a successful modern economy. Social organisation and institution building are also important. If British industry is to be successful in the knowledge-intensive industries of the future, action on a number of fronts will have to be taken by government in addition to improving incentives and removing unnecessary regulations. Undoubtedly the most important is the reform of our educational and training systems.

Education for Wealth Creation

Education and training can make a vital contribution to economic growth. The industrial success of Japan and Germany can in part be attributed to their first-rate systems of educating and training craftsmen, technicians and technologists. To be successful modern economies require a mass well-educated labour force. A small highly-educated elite is not sufficient. If blue-collar workers are to be taught to programme robots, they need to have a high-quality education.

It is also clear that major flaws in the British system of education and training have had a harmful effect on British industry. This adverse impact takes two forms. First, survey evidence has repeatedly revealed that skilled labour is a critical bottleneck for industry. The Butcher Committee, for example, estimated in 1984 that there was a shortfall in the electronics sector of some 1,500 electronic engineers, and that this shortfall would rise to over 5,000 by 1988.

Secondly, the low level of competence of our industrial workforce clearly results in low productivity on the factory floor. A recent study by the National Institute of Economic and Social Research illustrates this point vividly (Daly, Hitchens and Wagner, 1985). The study looked at 45 matched firms in Britain and West Germany. In order to permit an easier understanding of the factors effecting efficiency, factories making simple products such as coil springs, screws, hydraulic valves and drill bits were chosen. Labour productivity was on average 63 per cent higher in the German factories, which is close to the figures derived from the Censuses of Production of the two countries, which show that German output per employee in manufacturing as a whole is about 50 per cent higher than in Britain, and about 80 per cent higher in mechanical engineering and vehicle production.

This substantial difference in productivity could not be attributed to the amount or age of machinery, the size of plant, the length of production runs or overmanning. What was clearly different between the two sets of companies was the level of skills. In fourteen of the sixteen British firms visited the production foremen had acquired their position purely as a result of experience on the factory floor. The German production foremen in all sixteen firms visited had passed examinations as craftsmen, and thirteen had also acquired the higher certificate of Meister (master craftsmen). Above the Meister level all the senior staff in the German factories were qualified engineers except in one case where he was a qualified technician.

In British firms such positions were held by people with a sales or financial background or by persons who had learnt on the job. The high level of skill in German factories led to the use of more sophisticated machinery, the better use of ancillary feeding devices and fewer breakdowns, with the result that labour productivity was significantly higher.

This lack of skills in British industry has been known for over a hundred years, but the political will has never existed to correct it. What needs to be done to put it right? Action is required in four areas. First, the Government needs to set clear standards for the educational system. At the present time clear standards are not set, and this leads not only to a major duplication of effort but also to endless arguments about what the standards should be, and whether or not they are being met. In countries such as Germany where standards are clearer, the performance is better (Prais and Wagner, 1985). The German school system appears to bring a much higher proportion of its school leavers up to a broadly-based intermediate level. In Germany about 28 per cent of pupils stay on until 18–19 and reach university entrance standards, compared with only 14 per cent in England. Equally, in Germany about a third of all pupils leave school having attained the equivalent of "O" level passes in at least four core subjects, compared with one in seven in England.

A particular area of concern is mathematics, which is a key

foundation for subsequent study in many technical and commercial studies ranging from complex circuitry for electricians to book-keeping. Studies show that German and Japanese pupils, particularly those in the lower half of the ability range, are well ahead of English pupils. At the age of sixteen English pupils lag by two or three years in their level of attainment. The Cockcroft Committee of Inquiry into the teaching of mathematics in schools gave considerable attention to a proposed curriculum for the bottom 40 per cent of pupils. But because of the decentralised nature of the English educational system its recommendations could not be imposed on English schools. The lack of qualified mathematics teachers would in any event have made it impossible.

The achievements of the German educational system do not appear to require more resources. Pupil–teacher ratios are similar and the proportion of G.D.P. absorbed by education appears to be lower. The curriculum in German schools is, however, better co-ordinated. This helps with the development of teaching materials, and there is a closer link between schools and vocational education. Furthermore, such an approach appears to benefit pupils in the lower half of the attainment spectrum who are currently most at risk of unemployment. In England by contrast a totally decentralised system has been accepted without challenge. As a result many of our children are simply not receiving the education they need to get jobs. We need to move towards a more centralised system of education, where at least there is a national curriculum with target attainment levels set for all ages, so that parents, teachers and pupils know what the system is expected to achieve.

Secondly, we need to make the education system much less specialised. The number of subjects studied in Japan for university entrance is eight to ten, in France it is seven, in Germany five, in the U.S.A. six, while in the U.K. it is typically three. As a result, children in England and Wales are forced to take decisions at 13 or 14 which radically reduce their career options. Leaving aside the illiberal nature of such a system, it almost certainly means that children take these critical decisions not because of the effect they will have on their future career but on the basis of what teacher they like or what subject they find interesting. In 1960 Germany changed its system and allowed children in what we would call the sixth form to specialise in any two subjects of their choice. They found, however, that this resulted in a shortage of students coming forward to study science and engineering. They, therefore, abandoned the experiment.

Early specialisation has a harmful effect on industry, which not only needs engineers and scientists who are literate and can speak foreign languages, but also financial and marketing executives who are numerate and can understand the technology underlying their products and the production processes which make them. But the urgently needed reform of "A" levels, which would require students to pass in a broader range of subjects, has not taken place. Instead the soft option of "A/S" levels, additional subjects which university admission tutors may or may not take into account, is being introduced. The U.K. should move instead to a system like the baccalaureat, which involves the study of five or six core subjects up to university level.

It might be thought that with the education system producing an inadequate product, the buyer of the product, the employer, would take steps to correct the problem by providing more training than in other countries. But the reverse is true. Education in Britain is less relevant to industry than in other countries. Nevertheless British employers spend less on training. On average, according to a recent Manpower Services Commission (MSC) survey, British employers were spending only 0.15 per cent of turnover on training compared with over 2 per cent of turnover by German employers and nearly 3 per cent by Japanese employers. The third area, therefore, where action is required is the vocational education training system.

In the last recession, the training of apprentices collapsed dramatically, the recruitment of apprentices falling from 100,000 in 1979 to 40,000 in 1983. The apprenticeship system was clearly out-of-date, being time-served rather than skills-tested, expensive and based on a narrow range of skills. Unfortunately, nothing has been put in its place. The Youth Training Scheme (YTS) is a major initiative, but the skill training component is too small. It is also too general, consisting of areas such as "life skills" and remedial education in "core" school subjects, rather than specific vocational skills.

A first step, therefore, is to give a much greater technical content to the first year of YTS.

YTS also deals only with school leavers for the first two years after they leave school. It needs to be incorporated into an effective national training scheme. Such a scheme would also need to be backed up with financial incentives given the reluctance of employers in the past to do enough training. One way of achieving this would be by means of a Training Incentive Scheme based on the idea of a remissable tax system.

Under such a scheme, companies that spent more on training than a pre-assessed level would have all their extra expenditure rebated from public funds, while any firm that spent less would have to pay a tax to the Treasury equal to its underspending. The level could be revised upwards each year, starting in the first year just above the current average. There could be different levels for each industry to allow for different training require-ments, or only one level as in France. The definition of training would be strict. For training to be included it would need to be transferable and externally tested, modular and open to adults as well as school leavers. It must involve set standards so that people have an incentive to become proficient and training qualifications are meaningful. It must be modular so that people in a period of rapid technological change can update their skills, and it must be open to adults because the speed of industrial change is now so great that the skills of the workforce cannot be adapted quickly enough simply by training the inflow of new recruits.

Finally, a national programme to raise the level of skills of British managers must be part of any attempt to revive the fortunes of the British economy. In recent years a number of remarkable turnarounds have taken place in British industry as the result of new professional management taking over com-panies, but still management training does not get the attention it deserves.

ICL, for example, was saved from bankruptcy by the efforts of Dr. Rob Wilmot and his new management team, while Courtaulds and Jaguar have both seen an upsurge in their fortunes as a result of new chief executives. In most cases these turnarounds have been accompanied by major management training programmes which have stretched far down the organisations. For example, between mid-1983 and the end of 1984 ICL spent £3m on management training, a full 10 per cent of its meagre profits. In the last three years nearly 2,000 of its top managers have been pushed through an ambitious management education programme to enable it to compete against its aggressive Japanese and American rivals.

But these are exceptional cases, and the general picture remains very gloomy. Currently only 7 per cent of Britain's two and a half million managers have a university degree. A further 7 per cent hold membership of a professional body as their highest qualification, and only 2 per cent have any kind of business degree or management qualification. Seven out of every ten managers in British industry get no training at all for their management role at any time during their careers. It is not surprising in these circumstances that British companies are unsuccessful in world markets. They are being run in most cases by amateurs, while they are competing against companies run by professionals.

In seeking to reform business education in this country there is not, however, a single model which we can copy. While each of our major competitors makes a greater investment in management education, there is a great diversity of approach to business education in different countries (Kempner, 1983/84). In the U.S.A. approximately one quarter of all undergraduates read business, and the annual output of MBA's (Master of Business Administration) is 70,000. In Japan, a very high proportion of young people obtain higher and further education compared to other countries: and on this base Japanese employers have built very effective company-based management education schemes, knowing that they will not lose people because of the concept of lifetime employment. Germany too does not have business schools, but a large number of engineers and technologists receive basic managerial education as part of their first degree programme. In France, there are some 35 Grandes Ecoles in the field of management.

Faced with this wealth of options what route should the U.K. take? First, we need to ensure that a much greater proportion of engineering graduates receive significant management education. This means that we will have to extend engineering degree courses, but few countries now believe that engineers can be properly educated in three years. In West Germany, an engineering degree takes five or six years, two of which are devoted to economics and management.

Secondly, we need to expand the output of undergraduate and postgraduate business courses, with a medium-term target of doubling them (from an output of about 8,000 per annum to 16,000 per annum). Distance learning could be used to help us achieve this target, and we must also look seriously at new modular courses which enable young people to mix more easily the acquisition of skills with work experience. At the same time we must make certain that business education concentrates more heavily on areas such as product development and production management where we need to achieve excellence again, rather than simply on financial and quantitative techniques which are easy to teach. We should always remember, however, that management training will only really have an impact to the extent that all large companies establish systematic management development programmes for all managers, and managers take personal responsibility for their own development.

The Targeting of Technological Resources

A second key component of "competitiveness" which needs to be brought up to world class standards is research and development (R. and D.). This is a clear case where the problem is one of a misallocation of resources rather than a low level of funds. While a great deal of glamour attaches to "high-technology industries", their output is only a small part of the total output of most countries. As a result they have only a limited impact on the overall standard of living, which is more dependent on the ability a country has to apply technology across all its economic activities. Technology policy needs, therefore, to concentrate more on the diffusion of technology throughout the economy rather than on the generation of new ideas.

The technology policies of different countries can be divided between those that are "diffusion-oriented" and those that are "mission-oriented" (Ergas, 1986). In "diffusion-oriented" countries resources are put into education, co-operative research and product standardisation, in order to upgrade the capacity of firms to use new technologies. West Germany, Switzerland and Sweden are typical of this approach. In "mission-oriented" countries on the other hand resources are allocated to major projects of national significance, often concerned with national defence. The U.S., the U.K. and France are good examples of this approach, while Japan has features of both groups.

"Diffusion-oriented" countries have by and large been economically successful over a wide range of mature industries. Though firms in these countries are smaller than their competitors overseas, they have been able to minimise any relative cost disadvantage by higher levels of specialisation. They have also been very successful in high quality segments of markets as a result of their high level of skills. In the case of engineering products, approximately 85 per cent of Swiss exports, 75 per cent of West Germany's exports, and 65 per cent of Swedish exports in 1970 had unit values above the average of their disaggregated product category. They have, to use Michael Porter's terminology, "differentiated" their products by high quality and reliability.

The Japanese have in recent years challenged this pattern of specialisation by using new electronics-based technologies. The Swiss watch industry and the West German machine-tool industries are good examples of their victims. But as soon as it became clear that the old industry structure could not survive, these industries have had enough skills to respond strongly.

The "mission-oriented" countries have as a whole been less successful than the "diffusion-oriented" ones. The U.S., because of its huge research budget and the mobility of its technical, managerial and financial assets, has achieved a competitive advantage in the early phases of new technological trajectories. The small high-technology companies in Massachusetts and California have used new technologies to produce innovative products, and in that way they have "differentiated" themselves from their competitors. However, the same labour mobility has limited the ability of U.S. companies to compete in industries where accumulated production skills are important, and as a result in recent years cost leadership has in many cases been lost to the Japanese.

The U.K. in particular has achieved few benefits from its "mission-oriented" approach to technology. Because of a lack of incentives, its major projects have been less successful than those in the U.S. and France, and they have also drawn resources away from commercial R. and D. while producing few spin-offs for the rest of the economy. The results have been described as a "sheltered workshop" type of economy, with a few heavily subsidised high-technology firms surrounded by a mass of firms which do not benefit from government R. and D. We have clearly got to alter our national technology policies so that they have a much greater impact across the whole of industry.

The proportion of G.N.P. allocated by goverment to R. and D. in the U.K. is not very different from that of our competitors, but the benefits we receive are much less. Specifically, two major criticisms can be made of the way it is spent. First, a very high proportion of it is allocated to defence R. and D. In 1984 49.6 per cent was allocated to defence R. and D. as compared with 31.3 per cent in France and 9.8 per cent in West Germany. Conversely, 8.6 per cent of government R. and D. was allocated to industrial production and technology in the U.K., whereas the comparable figures in West Germany and France were respectively 11.6 per cent and 11.7 per cent.

A very serious consequence of this allocation of resources is that the defence sector attracts skilled manpower from industry. At least 1 in 4 of the workforce classified as engaged in R. and D. activities are in defence-related areas (over 50 per cent of British scientists work in defence), and there is a problem of quality as well as quantity. Because of the relatively high salaries involved and the opportunity of working on sophisticated technology without having to worry about the demands of the market place, defence research undoubtedly attracts much of our best technical manpower.

The easy answer to this problem is to argue that UK should spend a substantially higher proportion of its resources on R. and D., given its substantial defence commitments, and in this way maintain a similar level of government civilian R. and D. as its industrial competitors. This would solve the quantitative problem but not the qualitative one. In any case, it is probably not a realistic option given the constraints on public expenditure. As part of any overall strategy for upgrading the structure of British industry a re-appraisal will have to be made of the level of technological resources going into defence.

The second criticism of the allocation of R. and D. resources in the U.K. is that the industrial R. and D. budget has been biased towards the "big science" projects of nuclear energy and aerospace, with relatively small sums being allocated to helping incremental innovation directed towards market needs. Also the government's R. and D. efforts have almost exclusively been concerned with doing research rather than with technology transfer and the diffusion of new technology throughout the economy.

There are three major changes which need to be made to improve the contribution of government R. and D. to the upgrading of the structure of British industry. First, the R. and D. effort needs to be more clearly aligned with industrial objectives. This should involve not only allocating funds to new high technology industries but also to mature industries where there are technological opportunities for upgrading products and production methods. There will, of course, be people who will argue that such a task is impossible given the unpredictable nature of scientific research. But to see how it can be done one has only to look at the launching in Japan in 1981 of the "Next Generation Base Technologies R. and D. Programme" (Dore, 1983). Under this programme Y100bn (£270m) was allocated to 12 selected fields over a 10 year period. The areas of research chosen ranged from fine ceramics (£35m) and composite materials (£30m) to recombinant gene engineering (£27m) and three-dimensional integrated circuits (£24m).

There are two interesting points to be made about this programme. The first is the considerable volume of research which was done before the programme was launched. This included a list of 365 industrial problems which might be solved by research, a report on technology transfer, and a report on "New Industries of the 1980's", 17 industries identified as emerging or significantly expanding in the 1980's. An "informed respondents" opinion survey was also undertaken examining how Japan's technological expertise at that time, and as projected in five years' time, and its current price competitiveness, compared with the U.S., Europe and the N.I.C.s for 55 industrial fields. The second point of interest is that research objectives were specified in considerable detail. For example, quantitative targets for heat resistance, tensile strength, etc., were set for new materials. This careful approach to aligning research with the needs of industry is more likely to yield results than the totally random one which has been favoured by successive British governments. Large sums of money need not be spent on such schemes, but they need to be carefully targeted to focus the attention of industry on key areas of technology.

Secondly, more resources should be put into the diffusion of already known technology. This could take a number of forms. Department of Industry research establishments should concentrate more of their efforts on technology transfer than research and development. They should be required to seek industrial funding for their work, and where appropriate this should be on a consortium basis. The role they should be asked to play in Britain is similar to that played by organisations such as Battelle or the Stanford Research Institution in the USA, or ANVAR and ARIST in France.

Universities could also be encouraged to serve industry more directly: this requires a shift from deficit funding to incentive funding. If government wants universities to contribute more to industry, why doesn't it support the research which underlies such services by matching the level of funding that each university receives from industry? In this way it would make its support face a market test. We can also learn from the example of American universities, where it appears that the critical factor which aids the commercial exploitation of research is the willingness of universities to allow individual academics to develop their own commercial ventures while continuing as members of the university (Bullock, 1983). The earliest small research-based companies emerged in the 1930's and 1940's from the Massachusetts Institute of Technology and Stanford University, both of whom adopted such a supportive attitude to the commercial ventures of their academic staff.

More resources should also be put into advisory services to bring new technology and new business methods to the notice of businessmen. In agriculture such arrangements have long existed on the grounds that the individual farmer is not able to keep up with technological developments in his industry because farming is, to a great extent, organised in small units. But the same is true of many small businesses in manufacturing industries. In Japan, for example, there is a highly developed system for diffusing science and technology towards small and medium-sized firms through the 195 prefectural laboratories. Their primary aim is to produce technical assistance to industry, with the government financing half the laboratories' capital equipment and regional authorities and industry providing the rest.

Thirdly, in sectors where British industry has not kept up with international best practice, there should be an active campaign to import foreign technology whether through capital goods or licensing. For example, matching funds could be given to trade associations to encourage them to import technology in areas where British industry has lagged behind. Such an active campaign should be complemented by a deliberate effort to build up indigenous skills and R. and D. programmes. An ability to monitor technological developments throughout the world is an essential part of any effort to upgrade the structure of British industry.

Funds for Expansion

A third critical component of industrial success is an efficient system for channelling funds to industry. In the 1960's and 1970's it was argued by most financiers that they provided British industry with all the funds that it needed, and that, therefore, there was no need for change. Since the beginning of this decade, however, a large number of changes have taken place in the financial markets which have not only improved the situation, but have also demonstrated how financial markets can be altered in order to improve the flow of funds to industry. These changes can be taken further.

A key change was the launch in November 1980 of the Un-listed Securities Market (USM). It was essentially set up to counter a fall-off in the number of companies seeking quotations on the stock market in the mid-to-late 1970's; by the late seventies an average of only one company a month was coming to the market. Judged against this objective the USM, with its less stringent requirements and lower entry costs, has been a conspicuous success.

A recent count showed that 470 companies had come to the market so far, and had in the process raised over £850m for expansion. Of these companies, 61 had moved to a full listing, 38 had disappeared through mergers or acquisitions, and only a few had ceased to trade. This is a very successful record. Even more important, the setting-up of the USM has helped to increase the flow of venture capital to industry. It is much more attractive to be able to put funds into a small private business, knowing that it may be possible to sell the shares in five years when the company seeks a quotation on the USM, than to do so on the basis that the company will probably not seek a full quotation on the stock market for twenty years.

As a result there has been in recent years a very rapid growth in the supply of venture capital to industry. In 1979 the members of the British Venture Capital Association invested £20m. The comparable figure in 1985 was £324.6m. Of this figure £227.5m went to backing 517 UK businesses. It is also worth noting that employment in the 1,500 firms backed by venture capitalists since 1982 is around 250,000 and employment in these firms is thought to be growing at a rate of about 9 per cent per annum. British venture capital has grown from barely a dozen players at the launching of the USM to 113 fund management organisations, and Britain is the largest source of venture capital in Europe.

Mention should also be made of the Business Expansion Scheme (BES) which allows private investors to offset the full cost of buying shares in unquoted companies against their top marginal income tax rates up to a maximum of £40,000 annually.

The BES has been successful in a number of ways. It has drawn a large number of private individuals into small business investment, and it has raised the awareness of venture capital among City institutions. Many thousands of small investors put £147m into 787 companies in 1984/85, and several merchant banks have formed BES funds. However, a fairly small proportion of the funds has gone into companies seeking under £100,000 of funds. Although 65 per cent of the companies raising finance through a BES in 1984/85 obtained sums of less than £100,000, this accounted for only 10 per cent of the £147 million provided by the scheme in total. Also an extraordinarily high proportion of the funds have gone into the South-East of England. In 1983/84 nearly 40 per cent of BES investment went into the South-East: in 1984/85 this figure had risen to 63 per cent.

In the last five years significant improvements in the supply of funds to industry have, therefore, been made. But the level of investment required is still not appreciated by government, and there are still some significant gaps in the kind of funds available. British industry requires a higher rate of net investment to generate additional output than industry in other countries. This has led some economists and politicians to conclude that what is required is not a higher level of investment but more effective investment.

It is, of course, correct that British industry needs to invest more effectively. Many of the proposals we have put forward here have been designed with this objective in mind. As the comparison of British and German factories quoted at the beginning of this chapter shows, Britain suffers more from a lack of "soft productivity" gains associated with good management than it does from "hard productivity" gains which are due to better machines and equipment. But it is wrong to say that because we need to improve the effectiveness of capital investment, we don't also need to raise the level of investment.

Additional investment is required not only to bring industry up to international best-practice productivity, but also to create new capacity. GDP fell in this country by some 3 per cent between the 1979 peak and the 1981 trough, but has since recovered and passed the previous cyclical peak. The "competitiveness" of British industry in 1984 (measured on an index constructed from the LBS model, relating the ratio of unit labour costs to prices overseas) was better than in 1979. World trade had also grown by nearly 20 per cent in volume terms since 1979. It is, therefore, difficult to attribute to a lack of demand the fact that manufacturing output in 1984 was still some 10 per cent below 1979 levels, and that over the same period 1.6 million manufacturing jobs had been lost.

The explanation can, however, be found on the supply-side, for it would appear that between 1979 and 1983 some £15 billion of capital became uneconomic and was scrapped (Robinson, 1985). Assuming that the capital–output ratio in manufacturing industry is at its trend value of £15,300 per man, investment of £24.5 billion would be required to replace the 1.6 million jobs lost since 1979. Manufacturing investment in 1984 was only £5 billion. So to replace the 1.6 million jobs which have been lost since 1979 would require manufacturing investment to be double its present level for 5 years.

What action then can the government take to increase the level of capital investment, and what gaps exist in the kind of funds available to industry? A major flaw in the present financial system in the UK is the lack of any long-term fixed rate debt available at reasonable rates to small and medium-sized businesses. If a company is to expand rapidly using debt, then it needs to take on at least a proportion of that debt on fixed-rate terms, in order to protect itself from interest rate fluctuations. It also should not have to repay too much of the capital in the early years of the loan when the project financed by the loan is not producing a strong cash flow.

The UK corporate bond market has, however, been virtually non-existent since the early 1970's. This does not matter too much to the very largest companies who are well known abroad, and who can, therefore, raise medium-term fixed-rate funds from the Eurobond market. This market largely draws on investors from overseas, among whom are many small private investors who prefer to buy bonds issued by "household" names. A similar source of funds ought to be provided for small and medium-sized businesses. There are a number of ways this could be done, but probably the most effective would be a version of the "Industrial Development Bonds" which have been so successful in the USA.

The basic concept of "Industrial Development Bonds" is that bonds are issued by industrial companies, and individuals are encouraged to invest in them by being given tax exemption on the interest income on them. Such bonds should only be available to small and medium-sized companies and should be subject to approval either by the regional offices of the DTI or Regional Development Agencies. Because the interest from the bond would be tax free, companies would be able to borrow fixed-rate funds at a lower rate of interest. Only if some such kind of credit support is given will the fixed-interest bond market be available to small and medium-sized businesses. The Association of Corporate Treasurers recently published a survey of its members' attitudes to raising long-term fixed rate debt. In it they say "Interest relief, similar to that available on certain regional and European Community programmes, would be generally welcomed: in our view it would be the single most effective catalyst for a restoration of funding through the fixed interest market. . . .".

Two further points should be made about "Industrial Development Bonds". The first is that they should not be too costly to the Treasury: up to £60 million on an issue of £1 billion. Against this cost could be set the saving on unemployment benefit, and the benefit of Corporation Tax, VAT and other direct taxes flowing from any new jobs created. Secondly, they could have a substantial impact on employment. The Congressional Budget office has calculated that "Industrial Development Bonds" increased the American GNP between 1980 and 1985 by 4.75 per cent. A similar increase in the GNP of the UK would result in the creation of one million new jobs over the next five years.

The second area where the government should take action to increase the flow of funds to industry is that of small businesses. In spite of the increased availability of small company finance, businesses looking for less than £100,000 in equity capital are still likely to have a difficult time. The costs of appraising and monitoring investments are largely fixed, and as a result small ticket equity finance is usually considered unprofitable by venture capitalists. Also venture capital remains very much a London-based industry. According to Venture Economics approximately 60 per cent of venture capital last year went to London and the South-East, with the North getting a miserly 6 per cent. To cope with both these problems we would like to see government making loans at preferential rates of interest to BES and venture capital funds which focused on very small investments or investments in the poorer regions of the country.

Finally, there are a number of actions that the government could take to help small businesses, and in particular high-technology ones. There should, for example, be no Capital

Gains Tax on founders' shares and shares subscribed for new capital in unquoted companies at their first transaction, not only on investments made within BES but on those made outside it. Royalties on technical inventions could be made subject to Capital Gains Tax rather than to income tax, and 100 per cent first year depreciation allowances could be brought back for all start-up companies. Such moves would not cost large sums of money, but would have a significant favourable impact on the finances of small businesses, and increase substantially the rewards for setting them up.

A Partnership of Labour, Management and Shareholders

There are, of course, other major areas where the government should take action to improve the performance of industry, areas such as industrial standards, public procurement and intellectual property rights. But the policy changes we have suggested, and changes in these other areas, will only have a major impact if we can forge a new partnership of labour, management and shareholders. In recent years a better balance has been achieved in industrial relations law, and not much more will be achieved by tinkering with the system. A more positive approach is now required to achieve a greater community of interest among the different stakeholders in the firm. In the traditional economist's view of the company, its aim is simply to maximise the wealth of the shareholders. Equally, the employees wish simply to maximise their earnings. In such a system the interest of the shareholders and employees diverge totally. For example, the introduction of robots should be opposed by employees, as they will probably lose their jobs in order for the company to increase its profits.

But companies run on such lines will ultimately not be successful. Poor industrial relations are simply less efficient than good ones. We have to move to a new concept of the company, where it is seen as a partnership of labour, management and shareholders. This is why the concept of profit-sharing is so important, and why government should seek actively to encourage it. Schemes covering the whole workforce have so far not been widely introduced. Inland Revenue statistics for the number of schemes submitted from mid-1984 to September 1986 show only a small increase for profit-sharing from 588 to 778, and for savings-related schemes from 427 to 676. On the other hand, selective or executive schemes shot up from 162 to 2,483 over the same period. One of the best ways of encouraging wider profit-sharing would be to make the tax reliefs available under a Finance Act 1984 Share Option Scheme at least partly dependent on the company also having an all-employee scheme.

Only if shared objectives can be agreed by management, employees and shareholders, can companies attain their full potential. As Gary Hamel and C. K. Prahalad, experts on corporate strategy, have written:

"We believe that in many companies workers have been asked to take a disproportionate share of the blame for competitive failure. For example, in one company we know, management demanded a 40% wage package concession from hourly manufacturing employees which, if achieved, would bring hourly wage costs into line with Far Eastern competitors. The result was a long strike and, ultimately, a 20% wage concession from employees on the line. Yet direct labor costs in manufacturing accounted for less than 15% of total value-added. The company thus succeeded in demoralizing its entire workforce for the sake of a 3% total cost reduction (20% × 15%). And, if one looked closely, one found that the real cost advantage of Far East competitors derived not from lower hourly wages, but from the involvement of the workforce in systematically searching out opportunities for manufacturing savings, product enhancements, and diversification opportunities. Shared responsibility depends on a sense of reciprocal commitment and trust between employees and management. Most often, workers are asked to make a commitment to the goals of the enterprise without any matching commitment to them from top management— be it security of employment, gain sharing, or an ability to influence the direction of the business. A one-sided approach to regaining competitiveness prevents many companies from harnessing the intellectual horsepower of all employees in pursuit of more distinctive and long lasting competitive advantages."

A New Mix of Policies

The policies that we have put forward in this chapter, and the preceding two, are based on what we judge to be the best features of the successful industrial economies of the world, such as Japan, West Germany and the U.S.A. They have also been chosen because we think that they could easily be transferred to Britain. The Japanese concept of lifetime employment has many virtues, but it is difficult to see it being accepted easily in Britain today. Profit-sharing on the other hand has already been shown to work well in this country.

But could the mix of policies that we have proposed lead to a significant improvement in the performance of British industry? There is one piece of evidence that suggests that it could, and that is the exciting revival of industry in New England in the last decade. In 1975, unemployment in Massachusetts was 11.2 per cent, well above the average of the U.S. of 8.5 per cent. But the next decade saw a remarkable recovery. After losing 252,000 manufacturing jobs in the seven years to 1974, New England regained 222,000 in the next five. Service jobs also grew, but the main engine of growth were the high-tech companies lining the famous ring-road around Boston, Route 128. As a result of their growth, by 1984 unemployment was down to 4.5 per cent as compared with the national average of 7.5 per cent.

A number of factors led to the resurgence of industry. A major contribution was undoubtedly made by the Massachusetts High Technology Council set up by some of the high-tech companies in the area. In February 1979 they signed a "social contract" with the newly-elected governor, whereby they pledged to create 60,000 new jobs in the state if he would play his part in improving the tax climate. Tax cuts were made, so that in the state which was once called "Taxachusetts" personal taxes are now 5 per cent below the national average, and the member companies of the council also kept their side of the bargain by creating no less than 61,700 jobs for the state in the allotted time.

But other factors played a significant part. The Massachusetts Industrial Finance Agency used federal industrial development bonds to get old industries to re-equip, and to renovate city centre commercial property. Defence and space contracts picked up in the late 1970's. But the key factor was probably New England's remarkable concentration of educational and research establishments, including MIT and Harvard, combined with its vigorous banking and venture capital community. In 1983, for example, 15 per cent of U.S. venture capital funds, amounting to $1.5 billion, were controlled from Boston.

Finally, mention should be made of the Boston Compact, an initiative taken by the Boston business community which was worried by not having enough workers with basic skills such as languages, mathematics, computer technology and critical thinking. The deal struck with the school authorities in 1982 was simplicity itself. If the schools improved their performance industry would find the jobs. As a result in 1985, 93 per cent of all high school leavers were either in higher education or working full-time, and of the latter the Boston Compact had placed 87 per cent. New England has shown that action can be taken to revive industry. What New England has done in the last decade, Britain must do in the next.

As we showed in Chapter 1, macro-economic policies alone cannot reverse Britain's economic decline, although they could make a powerful contribution in conjunction with a significant increase in the performance of industry. And, as we have shown in the last three chapters, the most dynamic industrial countries in the world have deliberately and successfully adopted policies to raise their competitive advantage in world markets. There is no reason why we should not apply many of the same policies in this country. The scale of the benefits they will deliver will naturally depend on the determination with which they are pursued, but the sort of improvement in performance which it should be within our ability to attain could set the scene for a substantial reduction in unemployment. The scale of the potential benefits, if we can only get our act together, is discussed in the next chapter.

CHAPTER 5

Changing the Agenda

The policies set out in the last three chapters would have a substantial impact over a number of years on the ability of British industry to compete effectively in world markets. It is impossible to quantify the impact which each of the changes we have proposed would have on Britain's trading performance. But it is possible to illustrate the scale of the benefits which would accrue to the economy as a whole if, as a result of the policies advocated in this book, a significant rate of improvement in industry's competitive performance was achieved. Such an exercise also gives some indication of the scale of effort and resources which should be put behind policies to improve industrial performance.

The Scope for Improved Performance

The first point to make is that the scope for improved performance is considerable. The need for improvements in industry's ability to compete stretches right across the economy. Britain's competitive failure has not been restricted to one or two key sectors, but has been widespread as Table One, pages 80 and 81, shows.

This Table shows the performance of manufacturing industry divided into eight basic categories, and demonstrates what happened to the share of OECD exports achieved by each sector between 1973 and 1983. It also displays the performance of the same eight sectors on the basis of import penetration ratios.

Over the ten years only one sector of UK manufacturing unequivocally improved its performance in relation to equivalent activities in Britain's main competitors—Japan, the United States, Canada, France, Germany and Italy. This was Iron and Steel, which in absolute rather than relative terms cannot be presented as a success story.

Table Two, page 82, compares the UK's performance in the crucial high technology sectors with that achieved by Japan, the United States and Germany. In computers, the Japanese increased their export share by almost 250 per cent between 1973 and 1983—from 5.2 per cent to 18 per cent—whereas Britain saw its share fall by a third. Britain's relative performance fell back in other high-tech sectors too, although in aircraft and professional instruments the competitive position improved. Germany's advance in the aircraft sector was, however, spectacular.

These Tables bring out clearly that attempts to pick out one or two "key" sectors and pour resources into them—a policy of "picking winners"—would not constitute a particularly relevant response to the nature of Britain's economic problem. What is required is improved performance across the board. It is appropriate, therefore that many of the policies discussed in the main body of this book could be expected to improve the efficiency of manufacturing industry in general, although some would be particularly helpful to the development of high value-added, knowledge-intensive industries.

The needs of the country's principal exporters ought, however, to be given special consideration in designing a number of the policies we have recommended. If the objective of industrial policy is to improve the UK's trading performance, it is important to keep in mind that a large proportion of the country's exports are produced by a relatively small number of companies. Appendix I lists the top 100 exporters. These firms generated 49 per cent of the UK's total exports in 1985—£38 billion out of £78 billion. Leaving out the oil exporters, the remaining 89 firms accounted for 43 per cent of total visible exports—£27 billion out of £62 billion.

It is important to develop a dialogue between the government and the "core" trading companies, identifying constraints on performance and ensuring that the key policies are designed and implemented in such a way as to maximise their impact on

TABLE ONE: RELATIVE TRADE PERFORMANCE BY COUNTRY AND COMMODITY

		Japan	United States	Canada	France	Germany	Italy	United Kingdom
A. Exports shares (% of total OECD imports)								
"Advanced" electrical goods	1973	22.8	22.3	2.6	9.9	26.6	6.9	9.2
	1983	37.6	31.5	3.3	8.0	17.4	5.6	8.0
Other "advanced" goods	1973	5.6	60.7	5.0	11.6	22.4	5.2	16.5
	1983	7.1	59.8	4.6	13.4	27.7	6.1	18.8
Cars	1973	15.8	27.4	17.6	12.8	31.1	6.6	9.2
	1983	32.3	22.3	18.8	10.1	28.2	4.8	5.0
Machinery	1973	10.8	34.4	6.4	11.6	42.5	9.4	18.1
	1983	21.9	44.2	7.5	11.7	34.8	12.6	15.8
Iron and steel	1973	31.1	9.2	3.0	16.4	34.4	6.4	6.5
	1983	42.2	6.0	4.4	17.1	29.9	11.1	6.7
Chemicals, etc.	1973	10.1	27.7	5.2	10.2	25.7	5.4	8.8
	1983	7.6	25.4	7.0	12.6	23.9	7.2	10.6
Textiles, clothes, travel goods	1973	10.4	6.4	1.0	11.6	17.4	13.9	7.5
	1983	8.4	5.9	0.7	7.3	13.5	17.1	5.0
Other basic manufacturing	1973	5.1	12.3	9.1	9.7	21.1	5.3	9.3
	1983	7.7	14.5	9.1	10.8	22.1	7.9	8.7
Total manufacturing	1973	14.5	21.6	5.9	11.6	27.4	7.8	11.2
	1983	21.2	25.0	6.5	10.7	23.9	9.4	9.5

B. Import penetration ratios (% of GNP)

	Year							
"Advanced" electrical goods	1973	0.30	0.49	1.72	1.16	1.16	1.19	1.56
	1983	0.35	0.96	2.17	1.68	1.92	1.47	2.57
Other "advanced" goods	1973	0.21	0.09	0.75	0.47	0.33	0.45	0.53
	1983	0.33	0.16	0.84	0.59	1.13	0.68	0.91
Cars	1973	0.05	0.79	4.42	0.8	0.74	0.84	0.51
	1983	0.05	1.15	4.36	1.35	1.16	1.23	1.92
Machinery	1973	0.24	0.28	2.32	1.09	0.57	1.02	1.15
	1983	0.16	0.37	1.92	1.08	0.79	0.74	1.21
Iron and steel	1973	0.06	0.23	0.53	0.91	0.82	0.90	0.51
	1983	0.12	0.27	0.31	0.66	0.79	0.59	0.42
Chemicals, etc.	1973	0.17	0.12	0.29	0.52	0.42	0.52	0.54
	1983	0.33	0.22	0.43	0.86	0.88	0.89	0.73
Textiles, clothes, travel goods	1973	0.47	0.38	1.02	0.86	1.75	0.79	1.29
	1983	0.31	0.58	0.89	1.28	2.09	0.86	1.53
Other basic manufacturing	1973	0.72	0.48	1.37	1.76	1.85	1.74	2.47
	1983	0.56	0.62	1.24	2.07	2.41	1.85	2.52
Total manufacturing	1973	2.81	3.40	14.97	9.51	9.16	8.96	12.06
	1983	2.70	5.21	14.88	12.01	13.44	9.94	14.96

Source: OECD

81

TABLE TWO: TRADE SHARES IN ADVANCED
PRODUCTS

PRODUCT (SITC CODE)		EXPORT SHARES			
		Japan	USA	Germany	UK
Computers (752)	1978	5.2	37.3	15.2	15.7
	1983	18.0	38.7	12.9	10.5
Telecommunications	1973	26.5	34.2	25.8	12.3
equipment etc. (764)	1983	41.8	44.4	16.0	10.6
Sound and TV recorders	1973	90.6	10.0	13.2	8.9
(VTR etc.) (763)	1983	99.3	4.5	5.5	2.0
Pharmaceutical	1973	3.5	20.8	30.1	18.0
products (54)	1983	4.1	29.9	24.7	17.9
Aircraft (792)	1973	1.1	123.0	5.5	15.8
	1983	1.1	92.1	30.9	20.8
Professional, scientific	1973	81.3	37.2	33.1	14.3
and medical instruments (87)	1983	85.0	46.3	26.9	17.4

Source: OECD

these companies in particular, and through them on the balance of trade. To develop such a dialogue, however, government officials must have both a vision of the desirable overall structural development of the national economy, and a detailed knowledge about the products, markets and competitive dynamics of individual businesses. Businessmen will always be suspicious of government involvement in industry, but in countries such as Japan, Germany and France where the ability and relevant experience of government officials is very high their doubts have been overcome. The place, therefore, where management education needs to start is the Department of Trade and Industry.

Industrial Policy and the Economy: Assessing the Benefits

How much would the policies advocated in this book have to deliver in terms of improved trading performance in order to have a substantial impact on the progress of the economy and particularly on the most serious and apparently intractable current problem—the level of unemployment?

We asked the London Business School to tackle this question for us by using their computer model of the British economy to trace through the impact of a relatively modest improvement in industry's ability to compete in world markets on the main macro-economic variables—in particular the rate of growth, the rate of inflation and the level of unemployment.

The simulations were carried out in the context of the theoretical approach sketched out in Chapter 1. This suggested that an improved performance by industry could deliver a double boost to growth and employment. Growth and jobs would benefit directly from a higher rate of expansion in industry, as it took a higher share of export markets and reduced import penetration. In addition, however, a strengthening trade balance would permit the government to expand domestic demand, either through tax reductions or through increases in public spending, without precipitating a fall in the exchange rate. The proposition advanced in Chapter 1 was that in open economies it is via a change in the exchange rate that increases in domestic spending produce their main inflationary impact, so that it should be possible through policies designed to strengthen the balance of trade to provide a context in which the economy could successfully be expanded and unemployment brought down without unacceptable inflationary consequences. In terms of Diagram I, Chapter 1, the economy could be induced to advance along the line OK rather than along XR'.

To what extent does this general proposition in fact hold for the British economy? And to the extent that it does hold, how much more successful does industry need to be in order to enable significant improvements in growth and employment to be contrived without a deterioration in inflation?

We asked the London Business School to simulate the "double boost" which Chapter 1 postulated a more effective performance by industry would deliver. We modelled the impact of a particular level of improvement in the performance of British industry over five years. The improvement could in fact be either greater or less than the rate postulated and the policies we have proposed might require more than five years to achieve their full impact. But our purpose in presenting these simulations is not to make an economic forecast, but rather to illustrate the benefits which would accrue if Britain competed more successfully in world markets.

Part 1 of the exercise was to raise the rate of growth of exports by 1 per cent a year compared with the LBS's "base case" or central forecast (see Appendix II), and to decrease the rate of growth of imports by the same amount, these percentages standing as a proxy for the improved performance which industrial policies could generate. How readily such an improvement in performance could be contrived is not easy to judge. It would probably require a sustained national effort across the full range of policies advocated in this book. But our concern is to quantify what needs to be achieved.

Part 2 of the exercise was then to increase the government's public sector borrowing requirement (PSBR) to the extent required in each year to ensure that the exchange rate did not rise above the values projected in the base run. (In fact, the simulation came very close to replicating the exchange rate path of the base case, generating a series of exchange values just slightly below those in the base case.) So the government was assumed to take advantage of the leeway provided it by a strengthening trade balance and rising exchange rate to increase spending and bring unemployment down.

It was assumed that the funds raised by increased borrowing would be used not to finance tax cuts but to increase public sector employment, for example in health and education. In fact this increase in spending, costing an additional £1.6 billion per annum, generated an extra 40,000 public sector jobs per quarter. The results of the entire exercise are displayed in Table 3.

The proposed new policy combination as set out in Table 3 succeeds in raising the economy's GDP by 4 per cent compared with the base case. More than a million extra jobs are created over the period 1987–92, a number which could be increased substantially by more careful targeting of the public spending injection. ***This is achieved without any significant increase in the rate of inflation.*** For Britain the line OK is evidently flat for a considerable distance if exchange rate stability can be maintained in this way.

84

TABLE THREE: SIMULATED IMPACT OF PROPOSED
INDUSTRIAL/FISCAL POLICY COMBINATION

Differences from base case	1987	1990	1992
Output (GDP) %	+0.4	+2.6	+3.9
Retail Price Index %	0.0	+0.4	+1.7
(Inflation)			
Employment (m)	+0.10	+0.70	+1.12
Unemployment (m)	−0.08	−0.48	−0.73
Balance of Payments			
current account (£bn)	+0.09	−1.24	−3.36
& as % of GDP	0.0	+0.5	+1.2
PSBR (£bn)	0.00	−0.59	−1.3

(− means lower PSBR)

The computer simulations strongly support the central contentions of the book:

(1) that improved trading success would create the conditions in which expansion could take place and unemployment be brought down without additional inflation:

(2) that the rate of improvement in industrial performance necessary to deliver substantial benefits in terms of improved output and reduced unemployment ought with a determined effort to be attainable: and

(3) that a major effort in terms of time and resources to raise the competitive performance of industry is likely to be fully justified in terms of the scale of benefits accruing to the economy as a whole.

We also asked the London Business School to simulate "co-ordinated expansion", the other main policy option identified in Chapter 1, as offering a reasonable prospect of enhanced growth without unacceptable inflationary consequences. It was assumed that the countries in the European Community expanded together, resulting in an increase in monetary growth of 3 per cent per annum above the base case. In the UK, the expansion took the form of a rise of 2½ per cent p.a. in public sector employment, costing an extra £1.2bn per annum. The results are seen in Table Four.

TABLE FOUR: SIMULATED IMPACT OF PROPOSED
CO-ORDINATED EXPANSION

Differences from base case	1987	1990	1992
Output (GDP) %	+0.3	+1.8	+2.2
RPI (inflation) %	+0.1	+2.7	+6.3
Employment (m)	+0.12	+0.60	+0.88
Unemployment (m)	−0.09	−0.41	−0.58
Balance of Payments			
current account (£bn)	−0.76	−1.71	−3.25
(& as % of GDP)	+0.3	+0.7	+1.2
PSBR (£bn)	+0.21	−0.28	−0.11

The simulation results suggest that co-ordinated expansion could present an attractive trade-off for the UK between inflation and unemployment, but would need to be accompanied by "industrial policies" of the type set out in this book, aimed at improving the economy's capacity to supply, so as to ensure that the rise in inflation emerging towards the end of the five year period did not in fact materialise. In this particular case employment rises over the five years by some 850,000 with inflation rising significantly only towards the end of the period. A "two-handed" policy aimed at raising the economy's supply potential along with demand would help to mitigate this latter effect.

Co-ordinated expansion, therefore, seems to constitute an option which should be pursued with vigour by any British government. But the industrial policy simulations were themselves more impressive, since they suggest that by this route it should be possible to achieve a major increase in employment without any significant cost in terms of increased inflation. Industrial policies also have the advantage that they need not depend on the co-operation of foreign governments. The simulations therefore bear out the theoretical view suggested in Chapter 1 that policies to improve the competitiveness of industry in international markets should have top priority, although worthwhile gains could also be made if for example the countries of the European Community finally managed to design complementary expansionary policies, whether fiscal or monetary. Indeed, the two types of approach need not be regarded as mutually exclusive, but could usefully be pursued in tandem.

The policies put forward in this book represent the only realistic way of turning round the fortunes of industry and combining falling unemployment with price stability over the longer term. It has been amply demonstrated in recent years that simply exposing industry to market forces, without at the same time developing policies which are capable of improving its ability to supply increases in demand, is not sufficient to generate a significant advance against foreign competition. It is equally obvious that centralised planning does not provide a credible alternative. What remains is a set of policies organised and implemented by the government to improve industry's ability to compete and to accelerate the movement of resources within the economy from low value-added to high value-added activities.

In fact, policies designed to accelerate the responsiveness of industry to market developments will not only generate the benefits spelled out by the London Business School's simulations, but will also raise the economy's growth rate by producing a more rapid reallocation of resources from less to more productive sectors. The gains from more rapid reallocations are not captured by conventional macro-economic models and would therefore be additional to those which we attempted to capture by means of the illustrative simulations above. They may nevertheless be substantial.

Changing the Agenda

Many of the reforms proposed in this book are not new. Indeed, it is striking that even where major deficiencies in the British economic and social systems have been widely recognised over many years, little progress has been made towards remedying them. The low level of education and training of the British labour force has been known and written about for over a hundred years, but action has not been taken to raise it up to world standards. The poor allocation of Britain's R. and D. has been commentated on for over a decade, but the situation has got worse rather than better. In making recommendations about what needs to be done in the future, we must ask why it is that so little has been achieved in many of the areas discussed over recent years.

In our view, this lamentable state of affairs can largely be put down to three things.

First, the degree of consensus required to allow policies to be developed and consistently applied over an extended period has been notably absent from the British political debate. The industrial agenda has been dominated by taxation, nationalisation and industrial relations, because these are the areas where clear class interests are thought to be at stake. Attempts to improve trade and competition policy, to raise the level of education and skills of the workforce, or to allocate more R. and D. resources to industry, have always taken second place in the minds of the politicians. When, for example, education has appeared on the political agenda, it has been turned into a matter of class interest. While the politicians have obsessively debated the merits of independent schools versus state schools, and the value of comprehensive schools as compared with grammar schools, relative standards have steadily declined.

None of this has been true of our main competitors. Both Japan and Germany, for example, in their different ways have enjoyed the benefits of continuity of policy in relation to industry and the areas of policy impinging on its performance. In our view, electoral reform—a switch to proportional representation—is required in Britain to drive politics to the centre (the German experience), and provide the stable political framework which is necessary if a sustained assault is to be mounted on the basic problems we have identified.

Secondly, sustained progress has not been made in the past because policy-makers have lacked an intellectual framework within which to identify the types of structural development in the economy which are desirable, and thus the kind of intervention which is likely to promote, rather than retard, the country's prosperity. What is now required is a transformation of the frame of mind of the main policy-makers in the principal economic departments. In the 1930's, when the economy was suffering from a deficiency of demand, administrators and politicians needed to be given a "mental map" of the workings of the macro-economy, which was provided by the categories of national accounting, to enable them to design and pursue Keynesian policies. They now need to become just as familiar with the changing structure of the supply side of the economy. Just as nowadays policy-makers are continuously aware of trends in the balance of payments, public sector borrowing, the monetary aggregates, and so on, in future they should have as clear a picture of the sectors of the economy which are growing, the sectors declining, the changing trends in world markets, the extent to which the economy is adapting to them, and the policies which may be required to accelerate the process of adaptation to those trends.

The beginnings in the crudest possible form, of the development of the sort of "mental map" which is required to guide the design and implementation of industrial policies, were provided in the "diamond diagrams" in Chapter 2, which gave a simple illustration of the structural changes currently constituting economic development in the modern world and the direction in which the current pattern of activities in the economy need to change. Many of the policies laid out earlier in this book need to be informed by a more sophisticated version of this type of approach if they are to be designed with maximum effect on the country's trading performance.

Thirdly, government policies have not been co-ordinated in pursuit of industrial objectives. If economic gains of the types we have discussed—the improvements in efficiency leading to a stronger trade performance and also the dynamic gains from a more speedy reallocation of resources—are to be made and indeed maximised, "industrial policy", by which we mean a whole range of concerns in the public domain—from competition policy through taxation, the supply of finance, public procurement policies and the whole system of education and skill training—needs to be brought to centre stage and made the focus of the government's concerns. The spotlight must move from macro-economic policy, which seeks to keep demand in reasonable balance with supply at acceptable inflation rates, to the policies required to improve industry's capacity to supply.

In bringing together policies across such a wide area of public life and focusing them on the urgent and overriding need to raise industrial performance, two changes would be helpful.

First, the government should produce a long term "strategy

for industry" encapsulating the outcome of its analysis of the directions in which the structure of the economy needs to develop. This should be in a similar form to the periodic "visions" produced by the Industrial Structure Council of MITI in Japan. These "visions" seek to analyse how changes in technology and human needs are going to alter the industrial structure of the country, and what action needs to be taken as a result. A "vision" is not a long range plan, but rather a strategic look at where Japan should be going, mapping out the action necessary to correct its problems and take advantage of its opportunities.

Such strategic thinking is valuable for two reasons. One, it is a way of pulling together the policies of different government departments and making them support the single objective of improving the performance of industry; two, it is a way of stimulating a public debate about the strengths and weaknesses of the country's position. At a time when the strategic thinking of many British businesses is so poor, this is one way of trying to raise their awareness of the issues they need to consider.

Secondly, there need to be changes in the machinery of government to ensure that industrial policies developed to fulfil the industrial strategy are, in fact, implemented by the range of government departments concerned. One way of achieving this objective could be to establish a new Industrial Policy Cabinet Committee (IPCC) chaired by the Prime Minister, having on it all those departments whose policies have a direct bearing on industry (DTI, Treasury, Employment, Education, Environment, Defence). This Committee would undertake the task of agreeing the overall strategy, put forward by the DTI, identifying where policy changes need to be made in relevant government departments, and making certain that the agreed policy changes were implemented.

It may be, however, that the Cabinet Office secretariat would not be sufficiently weighty to achieve these objectives, faced with the inertia, vested interests and established thought patterns of large government departments. The strategy would need the backing of a powerful existing department with adequate resources to co-ordinate inputs from the different departments concerned in line with the strategy developed by the DTI, and to pursue the strategy's implementation at all levels of the Whitehall decision-taking structure.

On the British system of government, the most powerful department is the Treasury. Thus, there is a strong case for expanding the scope of the Treasury to incorporate not only finance and public expenditure allocation and control as at present, but also responsibility for drawing together, pursuing and monitoring the strategy for economic development.

Such an arrangement would have the further advantage that short-term economic management, and decisions on the allocation of resources for public spending, would more readily be made consistent with the industrial policies. If the Treasury were expanded into a new Department of Economics, the Secretary of State responsible for the new department would have a broader vision than the present Chancellor of the Exchequer. Thus, longer-term industrial considerations would make themselves felt on the Treasury's existing functions. The central point, however, is that the power of the Treasury in relation to public spending decisions, if deployed in support of the industrial policies, could be the crucial factor in determining that these policies were in fact implemented.

Finally, the objective of this book has not been simply to list a number of policies which if implemented could in some sense "solve" Britain's economic problems—though we do think the policies listed here could enable a substantial advance to be made in terms of non-inflationary growth—but to initiate a debate which might lead to a complete change of approach towards the fundamental problems of the economy and a co-operative effort to achieve competitive success in the markets of the world.

Our hope is that, once the conceptual framework is clear and the scale of the benefits to be gained from a sustained competitive improvement begin to be appreciated, a flood of ideas to achieve ambitious industrial objectives will emerge which go well beyond the discussion in this book. It has first to be grasped that competitive success is the key to full employment without inflation, and that public policies, properly organised, can assist industry to be more successful, and then the rest will follow. It may take some time, but Keynes was surely right when he said that: "the power of vested interests is vastly exaggerated compared with the gradual encroachment of ideas—not, indeed, immediately, but after a certain interval".

Appendix I

THE TOP 100 EXPORTERS 1985

Ranking 1985	1984	Company	Exports 1985 (£m)	% of UK t/o	Exports 1984 (£m)	% of UK t/o	Change % 84/85	UK Employees 1985 (No.)
1	1	BP	5,742	31.4	5,257	27.8	9.2	29,450
2	3	ICI	2,998	50.0	2,835	47.6	5.7	57,200
3	4	Shell UK	2,332	32.3	2,591	32.0	–10.0	15,558
4	2	Esso UK	2,282.8	52.0	3,216.3	60.0	–29.0	5,803
5	5	British Aerospace	1,623.3	61.3	1,564	63.4	3.8	75,800
6	7	IBM	1,582	52.0	1,175	50.0	34.6	18,798
7	6	GEC	1,236	34.0	1,209	35.9	2.2	127,460
8	8	Ford UK	1,035	26.2	980	26.7	5.6	51,200
9	9	British Steel	936	26.7	887	23.7	5.5	54,200
10	11	Conoco	876	42.6	823	42.0	6.4	1,476
11	10	Rover Group	764	32.5	598	30.7	27.8	67,562
12	14	Rolls-Royce	712	44.5	519	36.8	37.2	41,700
13	12	Texaco	701.7	28.9	686	20.5	2.3	2,987
14	(—)	Britoil	692	38.5	511	33.0	26.1	2,759
15	39	Mobil Oil	630	28.6	207	11.6	—	2,600
16	13	Jaguar Cars	503	79.4	408.5	79.0	23.1	10,440
17	15	Distillers	490	63.3	473	64.0	3.6	12,000
18	18	BAT Industries	424	25.2	407	17.3	4.2	25,389
19	16	Massey Ferguson	421.1	69.0	450.6	72.3	–6.5	11,867

20	19	Unilever	418	11.1	400	11.1	4.5	60,000
21	17	Courtaulds	384	28.2	442	32.2	−13.1	48,000
22	21	Johnson Matthey	375	51.9	354	54.2	5.9	5,179
23	22	Hawker Siddeley	336	21.0	336	21.0	0.0	26,100
24	20	STC	334	26.1	365	28.4	−8.5	34,300
25	27	Glaxo	332	59.3	261.8	57.3	26.8	13,463
26	23	Rothmans International	319	61.9	324	21.4	−1.5	5,260
27	(—)	Gulf Oil	315.6	55.1	282.8	56.5	11.6	753
28	25	Lucas	315	21.0	278	31.5	13.0	46,854
29	24	Racal Electronics	313.6	48.1	310	28.0	1.2	15,835
30	36	Kodak	307.8	53.4	261.9	50.9	17.5	7,921
31	29	Philips	292.9	24.6	239.6	22.9	22.2	21,994
32	(—)	Tenneco Europe	275.2	40.6	283.3	44.5	−2.9	9,766
33	31	BICC	275	23.3	231	22.2	19.0	46,419
34	26	Monsanto	268.3	65.3	264	66.2	1.6	1,740
35	34	Petrofina UK	259.9	23.5	217.1	17.9	19.5	1,633
36	41	Thorn EMI	247.1	12.3	203.3	11.8	21.5	69,034
37	33	INCO Europe	241.9	62.6	219.1	63.0	10.4	3,832
38	53	NEI	238	37.3	129	20.4	84.5	22,495
39	28	Rank Xerox	225	12.5	250	14.7	−10.0	8,000
40	39	Ciba-Geigy	224	37.8	207	36.5	8.2	7,066
41	37	Vickers	223.7	49.3	213	47.6	5.0	12,351
42	56	BTR	220	12.1	142.2	9.9	54.7	48,000
43	38	GKN	209	19.6	212	20.2	−1.4	27,200
44	46	Pearson	206	31.3	176	31.2	17.0	24,585
45	52	Beecham Group	193.1	22.7	154.9	21.2	24.7	15,700
46	30	British Shipbuilders	186.1	21.5	232.7	26.2	−20.0	40,785
47	51	Babcock International	185.8	61.3	160.7	57.9	15.6	13,774
48	41	Esso Chemicals	185	38.5	203.3	46.6	−9.0	1,380

Appendix I—cont.

Ranking 1985	1984	Company	Exports 1985 (£m)	% of UK t/o	Exports 1984 (£m)	% of UK t/o	Change % 84/85	UK Employees 1985 (No.)
49	66	Rio Tinto Zinc	181.4	13.0	116.1	2.0	56.2	18,000
50	57	De La Rue	178.3	71.7	141.9	52.2	25.7	6,586
51	47	English China Clays	175.1	30.6	165.2	35.5	6.0	12,473
52	54	Wellcome Foundation	173.7	60.7	143	59.0	21.5	6,514
53	55	London & Scots Marine Oil	170.4	71.7	142.3	68.9	19.7	136
54	50	Cummins Engine	168.6	67.1	161.2	71.5	4.6	4,642
55	61	British Alcan Aluminium	163.6	28.0	134	21.5	22.1	11,084
56	60	TI Group	160.5	28.1	134.6	24.6	19.2	22,000
57	80	Coats Viyella	157.2	14.9	87.6	8.2	79.5	45,500
58	(—)	Amoco UK	155.4	27.2	109.1	22.8	42.4	1,158
59	43	Davy	151.6	54.0	201	61.4	−24.6	6,000
60	62	Grand Metropolitan	150.8	4.7	132.5	4.4	13.8	95,200
61	(—)	A. H. Philpot & Sons	149	76.0	110.4	70.8	35.0	161
62	58	Caterpillar Tractor	147.5	86.1	137.2	88.4	7.5	1,806
63	69	Short Brothers	142	70.6	115	71.9	23.5	6,587
64	64	Seagram Distillers	140.5	48.3	131.8	44.1	6.6	1,944
65	70	Ferranti	138.1	37.2	112	36.7	23.3	19,117
66	44	John Brown	138	53.5	176.8	50.2	−21.9	5,894
67	75	J. C. Bamford	131.9	66.6	96.1	62.5	37.3	1,314
68	(—)	Pirelli UK	129.4	33.1	119.6	34.2	8.2	7,086
69	49	Plessey	128.8	11.7	163.3	16.7	−21.1	29,724
70	(—)	British Nuclear Fuels	127.6	23.4	90.5	19.7	41.0	16,000
71	63	Assoc. Octel	123.9	72.0	132.3	75.0	−6.3	2,409
72	68	IMI	123	30.5	115	23.0	7.0	14,524

94

73	59	Reed International	120	9.3	135	8.9	-11.1	24,400
74	86	Portals	120	50.0	78.3	55.1	53.3	4,148
75	85	Ingersoll Rand	118.7	70.7	79.6	60.9	49.1	3,285
76	72	Pilkington	116.4	25.2	106.3	22.5	9.5	16,700
77	78	Metal Box	116	19.6	89.3	15.4	29.9	18,662
78	(—)	Hewlett Packard	113.6	32.1	61.9	21.1	83.6	3,446
79	76	Simon Engineering	111.3	51.2	92	45.5	21.0	6,669
80	79	Lilly Industries	107.4	61.5	89.1	58.5	20.5	2,384
81	77	AE	105	38.2	91.7	47.3	14.5	14,500
82	74	May & Baker	104	34.9	101	36.2	3.0	2,339
83	73	Michelin Tyre	99.7	19.9	101.2	22.4	-1.5	12,531
84	83	Du Pont	99.6	27.7	83.2	27.6	19.7	2,058
85	(—)	Dowty	97.6	21.1	90.5	22.5	7.8	12,688
86	100	Bedford Commercial Vehicles	97.2	31.5	57.3	17.1	69.6	7,442
87	(—)	Baker Perkins	96.6	72.5	70.3	68.2	37.4	3,500
88	32	British Coal	96	4.8	224	4.8	-57.1	221,298
89	84	Smiths Industries	96	40.2	82	34.6	17.1	8,600
90	89	Allied Lyons	95.9	7.7	74.1	3.6	29.4	60,530
91	81	Cadbury Schweppes	93.9	9.4	87.4	4.3	7.4	18,522
92	82	Marks & Spencer	92.7	3.2	84	3.2	10.4	35,892
93	(—)	Gallaher	90.1	7.3	80.3	7.1	9.4	24,482
94	(—)	FBC	88.2	62.5	69	54.0	27.8	1,766
95	45	Royal Ordnance Factories	85	22.1	176.2	11.4	-51.8	17,500
96	87	Turner & Newall	84.6	26.9	77	29.0	9.9	9,300
97	65	Westland	84.3	35.5	116.9	66.6	-27.9	11,087
98	90	The 600 Group	80.6	46.1	75	45.0	7.5	3,026
99	88	Delta	80.1	18.7	75.2	17.9	6.5	12,100
100	91	Rowntree Mackintosh	79.8	16.5	71.1	15.1	12.2	17,700

Adapted from: Financial Times 29.7.86

Appendix II

LONDON BUSINESS SCHOOL BASE: OCTOBER 1986

	1987	*1990*	*1992*
GDP (£bn) (1980 prices)	232.30	251.89	262.02
Growth (GDP) %	3.0	2.2	1.9
Inflation (RPI) %	3.5	4.1	1.7
Employment (m)	24.90	25.95	26.72
Unemployment (m)	3.16	3.02	2.86
Balance of Payment (£bn)			
current account	−2.36	−0.38	−0.72
(& as % of GDP)	0.7	0.1	0.2
PSBR (Fiscal year) (£bn)	7.82	3.08	0.82

RESULTS OF INDUSTRIAL POLICY – ACTUAL FIGURES

	1987	*1990*	*1992*
GDP (Output £bn) (1980 prices)	233.22	258.44	272.24
RPI (%)	3.5	4.5	3.4
Employment (m)	25.0	26.6	27.8
Unemployment (m)	3.08	2.54	2.13
Balance of Payments (£bn)	−2.27	−1.62	−4.08
& as % of GDP	0.7	0.4	0.8
PSBR (£bn)	7.82	2.49	+0.48

RESULTS OF INTERNATIONAL EXPANSION – ACTUAL FIGURES

	1987	*1990*	*1992*
GDP (Output £bn) (1980 prices)	233.00	256.42	267.78
RPI (%)	3.6	6.8	8.0
Employment (m)	25.0	26.5	27.6
Unemployment (m)	3.07	2.61	2.28
Balance of Payments (£bn)	−3.12	−2.10	−3.97
& as % of GDP	0.9	0.5	0.8
PSBR (£bn)	8.03	2.80	0.71

References

Baden Fuller, Dr. C. and R. Hill (1984). *Industry Strategies For Alleviating Excess Capacity: The Case of the Lazard Scheme For U.K. Steel Castings*. Centre for Business Strategy, London Business School.

Bank of England Quarterly Bulletin (March, 1985). "Services in the UK Economy".

Brech, Michael and Sharp, Margaret (1984). "Inward Investment: Policy Options for the United Kingdom". *Chatham House Papers 21*, Routledge & Kegan Paul, London.

Bruno, M. (with Jeffrey Sachs) (1986). *Economics of Worldwide Stagflation*. Blackwell.

Bullock, Matthew (1983). *Academic Enterprise, Industrial Innovation and the Development of High Technology Financing in the United States*. Brand Brothers & Co., London.

Daly, A., Hitchens, D. M. W. N. and Wagner, K. (February 1985). "Productivity, Machinery and Skills in a Sample of British and German Manufacturing Plants". *National Institute Economic Review*.

Dore, R. (1983). *A Case Study of Technology Forecasting in Japan – The Next Generation Base Technologies Development Programme*. The Technical Change Centre.

Employment Institute (May 1985). "We Can Cut Unemployment".

Ergas, Henry (1986). "Does Technology Policy Matter?" *Centre for European Policy Studies Papers, No. 29*.

—— (1984). "Why do Some Countries Innovate More Than Others?" *Centre for European Policy Studies Papers, No. 5*.

97

Fusfeld, Herbert I. and Haklisch, Carmela S. (November–December 1985). "Co-operative R. and D. for Competitors". *Harvard Business Review.*

Hamel, Gary and Prahalad, C. K. (July 1986). "Unexplored Routes to Competitive Revitalization". *Working Paper Series No. 14, Centre for Business Strategy*, London Business School.

Kempner, Thomas (Winter 1983/84). "Education for Management in Five Countries: Myth and Reality". *Journal of General Management*, vol. 9 No. 2.

Keynes, J. M. (1936). *The General Theory of Employment, Interest and Money.* Macmillan.

London Business School Economic Forecast (Autumn 1986). Economic Outlook, Gower Publishing.

Magaziner, Ira C. and Hout, Thomas M. (1980). *Japanese Industrial Policy*, pp. 22–26. Policy Studies Institute.

—— and Reich, Robert B. (1982). *Minding America's Business.* Harcourt Brace Jovanovich, New York and London.

Ohmae, Kenichi (1983). *The Mind of the Strategist.* Penguin Books.

Pavitt, Keith and Soete, Luc (1980). "Innovative Activities and Export Shares: Some Comparisons Between Industries and Countries". In Keith Pavitt (ed.), *Technical Innovation and British Economic Performance.* McMillan Press.

Pinder, John (July 1984). Our Industrial Competitors and the Management Gap: Europe, Japan, the N.I.C.'s and the New Technologies. *Policy Studies*, Volume 5, Part I.

Porter, Michael E. (1980). The Technological Dimension of Competitive Strategy. In Richard S. Rosenbloom (ed.), *Research on Technological Innovation, Management and Policy*, Volume I. JAI Press Inc., London. See also Porter, Michael E. *Competitive Strategy.* The Free Press, London.

Prais, S. J. and Wagner, Karin (May 1985). "Schooling Standards in England and Germany: Some Summary Comparisons Bearing on Economic Performance". *National Institute Economic Review.*

Report by the Association of Corporate Treasurers, A. (April 1985). 'The Role of Fixed Interest Debt in the Financing of British Industry".

Robinson, P. W. (May 1985). "Capacity Constraints, Real Wages and the Role of the Public Sector in Creating Jobs". *Fiscal Studies*, Volume 6, No. 2.

Rothwell, Roy (1980). "Innovation in Textile Machinery". In Keith Pavitt (ed.) *Technical Innovation and British Technical Performance*. McMillan Press.

Shinohara, Miyohei (1982). *Industrial Growth, Trade and Dynamic Patterns in the Japanese Economy*, pp. 24 and 25. University of Tokyo Press.

Stopford, John and Baden Fuller, Charles (1982). "A Note on the Future of Western European Acrylic Producers". *London Business School Note*.

Thurow, Lester C. (1985). *The Zero-Sum Solution*. pp. 270–272. Simon and Schuster.

Turner, Louis (June 1983). "The Newly Industrialising Countries: Growth and Prospects" from *A New Investment Era: An International Investment Symposium*. Jesus College Cambridge.